Cutting Across Africa

Cutting Across Africa

Alan Cutting

ISBN: 979-8-7645-8569-7

Contents

Acknowledgements

Among all the wonderful people across Africa who have accepted and taught me, forgiven and rescued me, driven and hosted me, three wise men stand out. Thank you so much, Francis, Wandy and Mellbin, and your families and teams, for receiving me so warmly and sincerely into your lives.

Glossary

Samaritan's Purse International

A Christian International Relief organisation, with headquarters in Boone, North Carolina. A sister agency to the Billy Graham Evangelistic Association. I was employed for almost fifteen years by the Samaritan's Purse UK office, from 2004 until 2018. Always working on overseas aspects of the Programmes and Projects Team, my roles included managing the international relationships of Operation Christmas Child, developing the Short-Term Teams programme, co-ordinating the Disaster Relief responses, and directing the Raising Families process. I continue to serve on their Disaster Assistance Response Team.

Operation Christmas Child

A well-known children's giftbox programme, which was birthed from Wrexham in 1990 and managed by Samaritan's Purse from 1992. During each of the four years I was directly involved (2004-2008), we sent over one million giftboxes every Christmas to marginalised children around the world. My task was to appoint, train and monitor a National Leadership Team in each of fifteen different countries, in order that 'the right box was placed into the hands of the right child at the right time and in the right spirit'.

Raising Families

A Church and Community Mobilisation process worked out in Africa and Central Asia. Its role was to envision, equip and mobilise local churches to commit to the twenty poorest or most marginalised families in their village or neighbourhood, and walk with them out of their ultra-poverty over a period of three years. Through the 3,002 churches we partnered with over the six years between 2012 and 2018, 59,681 families saw significant, practical, quantifiable improvements to their lives – sicknesses averted, children in school, crops in the field and food on the table, and during that time a reported 14,705 people came into a living relationship with God through Jesus Christ.

Introduction

For fifteen years I worked in the Programmes and Projects Department of the large international relief and development organisation, Samaritan's Purse. Although my colleagues and I were constantly travelling around the globe, we would do our best to have regular face to face team meetings back in the office in London. As a team, we got on really well together. But one thing we constantly disagreed on was how to calculate the number of different countries each of us had visited.

Some argued that as long as you left the airport you could count its country as visited. Others reasoned that you couldn't claim to have been to a country unless you had spent at least one night there. Although climate change considerations would turn this on its head, at the time we each regarded the most credible method of calculation to be the one that declared us personally the *most* travelled. Ruth, a young woman who grew up as a missionary kid and had travelled all her life, lobbied for a system whereby we were required to work out the number of countries we'd visited for each year of our lives. By this calculation, she claimed she was top of the pile. Not having had a full passport until I was thirty, I of course argued against this method. Chris, the leader of our team, was so tough about all this that we joked that his criteria for regarding a country as visited was whether or not one had given *birth* in it.

For the ongoing harmony and wellbeing of our team, an external, objective rationale was clearly needed. And I found one. It satisfied all my gnawing doubts, albeit a method that massages and elevates the numbers somewhat. Not only did it suggest that a country is deemed to have been visited just as the plane landed on the tarmac (thus enabling the inclusion of countries that we had only fleetingly visited in transit), but it also included disputed territories, exclaves, island groups and islands, as long as those islands were either 200 miles from the closest continental portion of its administering country, or had a population of more than 100,000. In that way, and as I write, there are currently 329 countries and territories on The Travelers' Century Club list.

I am clearly well along whatever spectrum it is that likes collecting things and making lists. The latter, I recently discovered, makes me a glazomaniac, *g*lazomania apparently being 'an unusual obsession, passion, or fascination with making lists.' You learn something every decade.

So, during the 2020 Covid lockdown, and with my flights to Iceland, Kyrgyzstan, and the Ionian Islands (yes, they count) cancelled, I had little to do and nowhere to go but to return to my list of countries and, adhering to these new, external and objective guidelines, calculated that I had visited 109 different countries and territories.

At the last count, twenty of them are in Africa, eighteen of which are featured in this book. The other two? Well, with the greatest respect to the runways of the international airports of Freetown in Sierra Leone and Lubumbashi in the Democratic Republic of the Congo, each of which I have briefly landed on and graced with my jetlagged presence, there is only so much one can say about tarmac.

I frequently outline the purpose of my visits and, particularly in the slightly longer chapters of Swaziland, Uganda, Rwanda and Zambia, I focus on the people I have worked alongside through the Raising Families programme I managed in those countries.

However, Cutting Across Africa is basically a traveller's story. From Tabarqah in the north to Eshowe in the south, and from Dakar in the west to

Zanzibar in the east, I write about the people I have met, the lives they lead, the journeys I have undertaken, the struggles I have endured, and the impressions I have been left with. So many memories, meetings, and memoirs; travels, thoughts, and impressions. Trips made mainly for work, but also occasionally for holidays and for visiting friends. Sometimes on my own, sometimes with a colleague or companion, and sometimes whilst leading a team. Conversations with Presidents, Patriarchs and Parliamentarians and, equally compelling, with the least, the last and the lost.

For all their diverse and often distinctive characteristics, I sincerely respect each of these nations, and my faltering attempts at humour are merely tongue in cheek. I am unashamedly Christian, and I have sought to pray for and listen well to their people, remain hungry to understand their cultures, and consider it a huge honour to have visited their lands. In advance of you reading this book, may I offer my sincere apologies for my *mzungu* naivety, for the barriers I have unwittingly constructed due to unconscious bias and the limitations of my worldview, and for the inevitable misunderstandings and errors I have made in my endeavours to comprehend so many diverse and exciting cultures.

How to put this together into cohesive chapters? Should I feature each country in alphabetical order? Or in order of the date of my first visit? Or by region? North to south, maybe, or west to east, or even clockwise around the continent. Should I perhaps categorise them according to the purpose for which I went? Plausible as each of these collations might be, I have settled for featuring each country and territory in the chronological order of the main experiences that I describe.

Tunisia

Let's get this clear from the outset. I'm not a natural when it comes to package tourism. For all the trips I've done around the world, mostly for work, but also on holidays, very few could be filed under the heading of 'package'. However, my first few visits to Africa were exactly that. Having decided one year in the 'nineties to stay on a tiny island off Tunisia, my first wife loved it so much that she wanted to go again and again. And again. We would fly, via a short stop in Tabarqah on the north Tunisian coast, down to the industrial town of Sfax, on the east coast. An ancient fishing port it may be, but my two lasting memories of Sfax were the phosphate processing factories, and the many thousands of empty plastic bottles that were strewn and left bobbling in the oily water around the ferry port.

From this inauspicious gateway to the Mediterranean we, and those we were packaged with, would take the ferry to the two small islands of Kerkennah. As one approaches Kerkennah it becomes obvious that it is really nothing much more than a flat and arid area of sand and scrubland, dotted with xerophytic flora such as saltbushes and dying palm trees. Seriously, it is a wonderful place to go for those who want to chill out and do nothing. It's just that I'm not very good at chilling out and doing nothing.

And so, on this particular visit, to our hotel, where we had booked a refurbished room. It was rather basic, leaving me to wonder whether it had ever been furbished in the first place. But basic is fine, and with its doors spilling out directly onto a glorious sandy beach, what more could one want?

In what have become the two classic ways of describing the size of something, Kerkennah is a little bigger than a football pitch, and a little smaller than Wales. More accurately, from end to end it's about 30km. One has to be quite creative to find things to do there, other than lying on the beach.

Once I hired a little motor scooter and, on a pint or so of petrol, rode from one end of the island to the other. And back. Another time I found a local football match to attend. And another time still we took a two-day trip back onto the mainland, and across the Sahara to the Algerian border. But more on that later.

I also took up the offer of having an hour's windsurfing lesson. *Surfing* lesson, perhaps, as, unusually, there was no wind. I managed to balance

OK and, at a stretch, to maintain two of the three basic positions on the board. No one actually used the word 'expert', but now that I was fully trained and qualified, I was entitled to take the thing out for an hour each day, without extra charge. I took up this generous offer a couple of days later. It was disastrous for me, and hilarious for the many onlookers. After coming off the wretched thing about 25 times, badly cutting my feet and bruising my legs, and travelling no more than a collective 25 meters, I gave up and went back to my room.

They used to say of the village I grew up in that the night life was never the same after the stamp machine broke. It was somewhat similar in Kerkennah. But the hotel did what it could to remedy this by hosting different forms of entertainment each evening. Now my self-consciousness is not something I'm particularly proud of, and having fellow Brits gawking at me on the beach all day was voyeuristically painful enough. My skinny white beach body was not an image that gendered much adoration from my fellow travellers, but I could just about cope with that. But the evening entertainment put the reserved introvert in me at great risk of having to *perform* in some grossly uncomfortable way, be it song or dance, under the cynical eye of those who'd already spent all day gossiping about my slender torso. Or so, in my insecurity, I had convinced myself. Consequently, by about 3 o'clock each afternoon, the very thought of the evening's entertainment began to consume my every thought with dread.

The quiz nights were fine. We even quietly won it one night, fair and square. And watching children do a talent show was tolerable as well. All it demanded from me was some occasional and polite applause. The same minimal response was required for the weird bloke who came to the hotel to earn his living by prancing around on a small bed of nails and broken glass.

But then there was the dancing night, when I was dragged rather than persuaded from my chair to take part, on the basis of the wildly erroneous declaration of, 'Come on, you know you love it really' from people who had never met me before. It was excruciating. As was the karaoke, although this time I managed to hide quite successfully in amongst an ensemble of about fifteen people who had decided, rather unoriginally, to belt out a raucous rendition of 'Dancing Queen'. We started badly, tailed off a bit in the middle, and the less said about the ending the better.

But it was actually the 'playing-cards bingo night' that I need most inner healing from. In a moment of unusual and over-optimistic confidence, I agreed to take over someone else's hand of cards when they suddenly became unwell. In all honesty, I didn't have much time to think about it. He had even less. So, I told him it wouldn't be a problem. Glad to help out. I thought it would be a bit like the quiz night. Just tuck in there quietly and don't make a fuss. Participate, but don't rock the boat. What could possibly go wrong?

Actually, as it turned out, I zipped through the cards quicker than anyone else. In that air-conditioned room of about one hundred players, mainly British tourists but some Tunisians, novice Alan had done it again. I'd won! And so, as apparently one does, I shouted 'bingo!' and, to sighs of defeat and scowls of resentment from those on nearby tables, I rose humbly to take my cards to the front desk for checking. "First time I've ever played," I told the caller, nonchalantly, as he checked my cards and prepared to present me with my 37 Dinah winnings. Oh, the glory.

I guess it was about then that the first seed of doubt crept in, a seed that rapidly grew into a gnawing, gripping sensation in my already volatile bowels. Something was wrong. Dreadfully wrong. The awful error of my ways was fully exposed as the caller apologetically explained to every tourist this side of

Cairo that the dork in front of him had mistaken the 8 of spades for the 8 of clubs. Well, how was I to know? They were called blackberries last time I played. The game collapsed, and with it Anglo-Arab relations. I'd messed up the whole evening's entertainment, for tourists and locals alike. Tensions rose, and world peace hung in the balance. Repentance was insufficient. A forfeit was required, I was told, before I could sit down. Diplomatically, albeit shakily, for my punishment I chose to sing, 'Show me the way to go home' and, to be fair, that did seem to do the trick. Gradually international relations began to stabilise.

Actually, kind people kept coming up to me afterwards to encourage me. They told me that that was the best laugh they'd had since watching some plonker falling off his surfboard the previous week. At least I had a different tee-shirt on that day. Maybe they won't ever find out.

Thus, I became even more convinced of what I already knew. Package holidays aren't really my thing. I clearly recall saying to my parents as a young child, "I don't like red and yellow holidays. I like green and brown holidays." I'm a traveller, to be sure, but I don't exactly thrive on beaches and entertainment.

But the holiday was redeemed by a two-day coach trip, which also included the use of various other modes of transport including a ferryboat, a pony and cart, a camel, and a four-wheel drive truck. After the ferry crossing to Sfax, we headed down to Gabes and on to Matmata. It is here that we visited some Berber troglodytes still living in caves in the mountains. By sunset we were riding camels into the Sahara, near the oasis town of Douz.

The following day we drove over the Atlas Mountains and crossed 'the largest salt-lake in North Africa' in Touzer. There we took a Land Cruiser up to the Algerian border, stopping at Chbika, Tamerza and Redeyef, before dropping back down the Atlas Mountains on a four-hour dash to catch the late afternoon ferry back to our island home.

A few miles beyond the town of Gasfa, which is famous for its pistachios, a red light flashed ominously on the coach's dashboard, a siren sounded, and the bus crunched to a halt. The driver gave it the benefit of a short rest but, even then, it would not start. We were stuck in the Sahara, 40 degrees and no shade, no air conditioning, no transport, and the last ferry of the day preparing to leave port. Now this really was turning into my sort of trip! After 15 minutes of our driver and guide head-scratching and arm-waving over the engine compartment, a local bus pulled up. It puffed, and it wheezed. But it worked. And it was stuffed full of Tunisians on their way to Sfax. All sixteen of us tourists managed to squeeze on board, slinging cases and bags onto the roof and our laps, and off we chugged. Locals, including a large family with a very elderly and badly crippled man and small children, were waived aside as we whizzed past isolated bus stops. There really was no more room on the bus. But to this day, I still anxiously wonder where those poor people spent that night. In Sfax, the bus driver caught the sense of urgency, and kindly changed his route in order to take us directly to the ferry terminal. We all madly grabbed our luggage off the roof (and in our haste, I fear, some of the locals' luggage as well), and jumped onto the ferry with moments to spare. Eight modes of transport and more than 800km. My wife, rather damning it with faint praise, reflectively confessed that she quite liked the trip. I absolutely loved it.

Mozambique

I usually make all my own travel arrangements, but occasionally I would be in the hands of others when it came to booking accommodation. To be honest, whoever was paying, I always preferred and felt more comfortable in quite modest accommodation and, when planning a work trip, developed a habit of requesting a 'simple, clean and safe' place to stay, adding in more recent days 'and one that has internet'. But my first visit to Mozambique was in my very early days of working with Samaritan's Purse International, and I was in the hands of their local office staff team who, as was their want, had booked me into Maputo's five-star Holiday Inn, with its glorious grounds of green lawns, graceful palms, and an infinity pool that gave way to the golden beach of the Indian Ocean.

I have two memories of that stay. One was of the Malawian National Football Team who were there to play their Mozambiquan counterparts and who, at breakfast, looked even more wide-eyed and overwhelmed by their lavish surroundings than I did.

The second memory still leaves a sour taste in my mouth. It was of the appalling way that some white, male, South African tourists treated the local staff. Arrogance in the extreme. I went onto the beach to calm down, and was soothed by the lapping of the waves, and distracted by the sight of fisherman landing their catch and selling it to waiting women, who would sell it on to their customers at a downtown market that evening.

My colleague and I were up early the following morning for our three-hour trip from Maputo to the tomato growing community of Chokwe, situated 230km north of the capital, on the south shore of the Limpopo River. With the salubrious Holiday Inn experience lost in the dust of our rear-view mirror and fading from our minds, we began to see a more intrinsic Mozambique. It was poor. Since independence in 1975 the country has been continually knocked back by civil war, by drought, by HIV/AIDS and by regular floods. At the time, communities were still recovering from the massive flooding disaster of 2000, which killed 700 people and affected 2 million lives. Chokwe was particularly hard hit; water surged down the Limpopo River flooding approximately 1,400 square kilometres of farmland. The heavy rainfall lasted for five weeks, thousands of cattle were lost, and thousands of people were made homeless. Chokwe was to be affected by at least four more major floods in the coming years, each of which further destroyed homes, roads, bridges and public buildings.

After we'd checked into the much more basic Limpopo Hotel, we took the truck to the river, and a boat over it, to Guija District. The town of Guija is sometimes known as Canicado. Here lived and worked some colleagues from our organisation, about half a dozen 'ex pats' (as they like to call themselves - I much prefer the more egalitarian expression 'foreigner' myself) - and a much larger number of locals. We spent the day meeting people and viewing FFW - 'Food for Work' - programmes out in the bush. Presently, the 'work' which community members undertook for 'food' was the development of a dyke, and the management of a ten-acre site of cassava and sweet potato which were harvested for seed multiplication. We ate rice, chicken and *xima* (or *chima* - a cornmeal porridge) for lunch, and rice, chicken, and coconut for tea. Many local households had been given a water filter for their homes and neighbourhoods, and we were given a demonstration of how these innovative filter systems worked. And we visited the warehouse where the food is stored.

Sun sets here at about 5pm, and by the time we'd eaten it was utterly dark. Pitch black on the ground that is, but with a magnificent canopy of southern hemisphere stars overhead. We picked and stumbled our way down the track to the Limpopo River by feeble torchlight and a million stars. This was where the very worst of the floods occurred in February 2000. Here, crocodiles live in the river, and the occasional hippo, so as we called and whistled over to the other bank, we trusted not only that there would still be a boatman there, but also that he would find us more quickly than the wildlife would. Someone whistled back, but whether or not that was Shangaan for, 'We're on our way', or for, 'You must be joking, mate. Come back tomorrow', we could not tell.

A nearby disturbance in the water punctured the silence. That splash was the only sound we heard for some time. But just as we were discussing contingency plans, my colleague spotted a dark shadow looming out of the blackness right in front of us. Two lads with a leaky wooden boat and a long punt had arrived for us. Extraordinarily, immediately the boat had arrived, other figures emerged from the darkness on our side of the river. Had they intuitively sensed the boat's arrival, or had they been there all the while?

It took just ten minutes for the lads to silently punt back to the Chokwe side of the river. Upon stepping across the boat to disembark, I accidentally stood on someone who, unbeknown to me, had been sleeping on the floor of the little craft. A further five minutes of groping our way along the dirt track, and a final five minutes of driving, and we were back at the relative civilisation of the Limpopo Hotel. As far as journeys go, now that's what I call fun.

The following morning, we journeyed across the Limpopo once more. Meeting up with some more staff members, we were bundled off in their Land Cruiser and headed north, further into Guija District. We spent the morning in the village of Nhampugnaune, attending the World Food Programme monthly food distribution, and visiting a couple of homes. While my colleagues looked into some more technical aspects of the programme, I took time out to meet Salomao Chicanequisso Cuinica, the Community Leader.

Nhampugnaune's 2,300 people are spread across four barrios or districts. Each barrio has a secretary who reports to Salomao. He was overseeing the distribution, ensuring equity amongst the twenty-five participant families. At least one family member has to work for a minimum of three hours a day on the Food for Work programme, employment such as building the dyke in order to access fields across a flood plain, or cultivating the seed multiplication initiative. In exchange, each participating family receives a monthly food package consisting of maize (75kg), yellow split peas or beans (7.5kg), and 3.7 litres of Soya bean oil.

Some families live on this alone - I'd just witnessed both their payday and their monthly shopping trip, all rolled into one. Other families have a little meat, I was told. Indeed, I saw the evidence of this myself. As I walked around the village, I saw one large fish cut open and drying on the straw roof of a mud house, and about 15-20 charcoaled rats waiting for preparation outside another. The empty Soya bean oil cans themselves come in useful. Six or eight of them had been beaten flat and made into the door of one family's little circular mud and thatch hut.

There is no electricity in the village, but the government has promised to supply it. When did they promise, I ask? Oh, years ago, came Salomao's reply. Malnutrition levels in Gaza are showing worrying levels of 11%. The official figure for HIV/AIDS in the country is 1.4m, with 13% of 15-49-year-olds living with the virus. But come to Gaza Province and the official figure becomes 19%, the highest infection levels in the country. Local district estimates put it at more like 50%.

The previous owner of Salomao's jeans clearly had an entirely different shape from him. His ancient vest was full of holes. I guess his attire reflected his financial status. Salomao Chicanequisso Cuinica was not a rich man. He also looked like a man on whose kindly shoulders rested many a care. An observant man, I thought, though a man of few words. But with the food distribution over, he was happy to tell this strange white visitor to his village something of his life and aspirations.

Appointed as Community Leader in 1976, just twelve months after independence, Salomao witnessed Mozambique's slide into civil war. The village of Nhampugnaune was on the front line. The fighting was bitter, and atrocities were committed on a massive and horrific scale. One of Salomao's early tasks was to lead his community to safety, across the Limpopo River to the nearby town of Chokwe. It was six years before they returned. Upon venturing back, Salomao re-established the village in a position he considered was far enough away from the river to protect it from flooding, but close enough to access the water for crop irrigation. It's a good place to be, he told me.

Droughts followed. Then floods. Either way the crops failed. Salomao couldn't remember the years. But he remembered 2000. While the West mopped its collective brow with relief over the fact that our computers had survived the Y2K scare, the inhabitants of Guija District had other things on their minds. On 27 February 2000, the Limpopo burst its banks. In the few hours that followed, 700 people died. A total of 2 million were affected. Around here, it is spoken of as 'the time of the floods'. Perhaps more accurately written as 'the Time of the Floods'. Capital T, capital F.

The flood water had stopped just short of the village Salomao had repositioned. There was no proud smile upon his face when he told me this, but I think maybe his shoulders went back just a little. His people were spared their lives. But of course, their harvest was not so fortunate. Yet another year of nil return.

So, my employers had opened a field office in Guija, where these days that handful of 'ex pats' and many local people are employed, providing simple and appropriate relief initiatives such as water filters, seed multiplication, food for work programmes and HIV/AIDS awareness training. The transition from relief to development is well under way. The handout is giving way to the hand up.

I asked Salomao what his major concerns were for the future of Nhampugnaune. His replies were clear, simple, and realistic. He wants a well for the school, in order to save the children from having to travel such a long way for water. And he looks forward to the day when each family in the village has a water filter.

I realised with a degree of embarrassment how Western my questions were. When were the worst drought years? He didn't remember the year. How many families in the village have a water filter now? He didn't know. Quite a few now, he thought. How often were people sick before they used the water filter compared with now? Again, he didn't know. All he knew was that they used to be sicker than they are now. Fair enough. So much for my quantifiable research!

Just before I left in the back of the 4WD, I gave Salomao a tiny token gift from the UK. And I realised he had come out of his shell a little. With his arm round a young lad's shoulder, his weary, burdened face gave way to a big smile. He raised his arms above his head and applauded our departing vehicle, rather like a substituted footballer acknowledges the crowd. Against the odds, over maize and rats, through conversation and respect, we'd connected somehow. But the next monthly shopping trip was still many moons away.

Senegal

I was due to visit Senegal only briefly, in order to meet my Ivorian colleague Edouard. From there we would travel on to The Gambia – note the definitive article - together, for a meeting with national church leaders. Our aim was to establish a National Leadership Team for the distribution of Operation Christmas Child giftboxes. By travelling via Senegal, I could meet with Edouard before the big meeting, and would also save my employers hundreds of pounds in airfares. Or so I thought. As things turned out, a six-hour delay at Heathrow, cancelled flights, missed connections, and eventually being rerouted from Rome to Lisbon all meant that my first glimpse of Dakar, Senegal was at 1am on a Wednesday morning in August 2005. This was, in fact, my first taste of West Africa.

My flight delays had little consequence to the schedule, however, as our onward flight to The Gambia was not due to depart Senegal until 6pm. Edouard and I therefore spent a quite leisurely breakfast of omelette, bread, and tea at the hotel, talking through our plan for the following day's meeting.

The hotel directly overlooked the breaking waves of the Atlantic Ocean as they completed their long journey onto the boulder-strewn shoreline of Africa's most westerly country. Compelling ambiance as this was, I was still eager to get out of the hotel and experience a little more of the city. When news came through that our evening flight had been cancelled, my experience of the city suddenly became a hurried dash between travel agents and car hire, airline, and coach companies. Edouard, far more familiar with the region than I, had a cunning plan. We would drive the 330km down to the border, either by bus or by hire car, and catch the ferry across the Gambia River to Banjul. Or even drive another 400km inland, through the night, to cross the first, most westerly bridge to The Gambia's south shore. In that way we could still arrive, albeit exhausted, in time for our meeting, a gathering that we had initiated, and one which senior church leaders from all over The Gambia had kindly agreed to attend.

While various travel agents strived to work out our best options, there was nothing we could do but wait. Edouard contacted an old friend who, on hearing we were in town, invited us to share a meal with his family in their second-floor apartment near central Dakar. Introductions were confusing. "Al-you," he said warmly, thrusting out his hand in greeting. It had sounded like a question.

"Yes," I replied, "Although most people call me Alan." He hesitated, and looked puzzled.

"No. Al-you. My name is Al-you." Not a great start.

Introductions - and embarrassed apologies - over, and while Al-you's wife was busy in the kitchen, Edouard and our host both promptly fell asleep in armchairs. The remainder of the floor space was then taken up by Al-you's other Sufi guest who, without a word of explanation to me, responded to the local *muezzin*'s recital of the *adhan* by laying out his mat and bowing prostrate on the floor, in the direction of Mecca. The only space left in the room for me was the window ledge, on which, despite feeling a little awkward in body (and in soul), I perched.

At least it gave me a great vista of Dakar street-life below, where children played, vendors called, rubbish trucks collected, builders built, and coal was delivered to the flat roof of a nearby house. Men and women, mostly in conservative Muslim dress, walked on street and pavement alike, boys and girls played and shouted, and young men sold petrol in plastic bottles. Young women gracefully walked with plastic baskets full of freshly washed clothes on their heads, before hanging them out to dry across roof tops, bringing an array of bright colour to the otherwise drab and dirty concrete building blocks. Later that day I would write in my diary, 'West Africa is vibrant and colourful, if also quite grubby and smelly. At least Dakar is. The people of French speaking Senegal are notably tall and elegant. Dakar teems with *Car Rapides*, yellow white and blue public minibuses. They have no glass in the windows and no doors, and young men hang out of their every orifice as they pollute their way across the city.'

My attention was drawn back indoors with the announcement that our meal was ready. The men awoke, the mat was rolled away, and in its place across the floor was laid a clean cream cloth. Cross-legged and with bare feet, we sat around the edges of the cloth, and were each given a spoon. Strictly using our right hand only, with the spoon and with our hands we dipped into the one large single dish; a base of rice, onto which a meat stew was lavishly placed. The edges of the dish were delicately ladened - adorned more accurately - with slices of hard-boiled eggs, tomatoes, and cucumbers.

Once replete, we drank an incredibly thick, sweet tea, and ate monkey bread pods from the magical and revered baobab tree. With six times more vitamin C than an orange, and 50% more calcium than spinach, these sweet and sour pods can be eaten raw or made into a juice. Its pulp helps prevent liver damage and hepatitis. But the value of the baobab tree does not end with its pods. Its bark is made into ropes and baskets, its roots are ground down and used both as a dye and as a remedy for malaria, its leaves calm fever, and oil extracted from its seeds relieves toothache. With such powers, I began to wonder if it could also get us to The Gambia.

Despite their best efforts, all the travel agents were facing the same two problems. The ferrymen were on strike, and the bridge had collapsed. Even if we drove down to the border, we would not be able to cross. Be it by air, by land, by water, or by baobab tree, we were now all but resigned to the fact that Banjul, and our meeting, were out of our reach. There was just a tiny chance that we could still catch an 8am flight, but we wouldn't know until early the following morning.

Back at the hotel, we did our best to contact key people over in Banjul, and plead with them to be patient with us. I hate being late, and I hate letting people down. And these were busy and important people who we had never met before. I was at least grateful that I had a bed for the night, albeit in the wrong country.

Another day of travelling frustration would follow. No call came to summon us to the airport for the 8am flight, so we went to the Dakar offices of Slok Air International to see what (if anything) was occurring. They were remorseful that they hadn't let us know (if we had known the morning flight had been cancelled once more, there was a very vague chance that we could have found another airline to take us) and so funded an alternative flight and personally took us in an air-conditioned Toyota to the offices of Air Senegal International, where we purchased two tickets for the 21.20 flight to Banjul.

This provided us with another, albeit unplanned, day in Dakar. While Edouard waited to take part in a conference call to Boone, North Carolina, I did some work in my room. That left us unsuspecting tourists a couple of hours in the afternoon, to jerk by clutch-less taxi into Dakar, where we attempted to go by ferry to Goree Island (famous for the export of slaves) on the Cap Vert peninsular. But with a late evening flight requiring us to be at the airport by 19.30, the ferry would not have got us back in time, so we settled for a shorter look round town. My repeated hint that I would like to go to Africa's most westerly tip was regarded with bemusement and negativity. Apparently, I didn't really want to do this at all! I realised how obsessed I am with quirky facts and geographical statistics, whereas the citizens of Dakar (even local taxi drivers) had no knowledge or interest of where the furthest west point actually was.

So, we went to the airport (ironically, this is within a few hundred meters of the western tip!) by 19.30.

"Sorry," we were told, "but the flight is delayed till 23.20. Have a free meal." At 23.00 it was clear that still no plane was available.

"Sorry, but the flight is delayed till 02.10. Have a free drink." As we eventually took off from Dakar, I looked at my watch. It was 02.52 on Friday morning. What I had thought would be a six hour stop over through Tuesday night had become a 50-hour city break. And I had yet to go on any of the three flights I had booked to get to The Gambia. Having left home at 8am on Tuesday, we arrived at our apartment near Banjul at 5am on Friday. Journey time: 69-hours!

The Gambia

Readers of the previous chapter will recall that I had travelled to The Gambia to meet with the senior leaders of the mainstream churches of this, the smallest mainland country in Africa. These leaders had agreed to meet with me and my Ivorian colleague Edouard to discuss the potential for the famous Christmas giftbox programme, Operation Christmas Child, to be established in their country. If all went well, two containers with over 14,000 gifts for the poorest children in The Gambia would arrive at Christmastime.

As flights from the UK were much cheaper to Dakar (Senegal) than to Banjul (The Gambia) and as Edouard was already in Dakar, we had arranged to meet there and travel to The Gambia together. This backfired on us, due to flight cancellations and a ferry strike, as I described in the previous chapter. We eventually arrived in The Gambia at 04.30 the morning *after* our scheduled meeting, and inevitably, some of those we had arranged to meet had had to return to their homes without meeting us.

About two thirds of these busy men – sixteen of them - and one busy woman had stayed on in Banjul to meet with us, a day late. Most were pastors, the vast majority of them being missionaries from Ghana and Nigeria. Apparently Gambian pastors are few and far between. We were received quite formally but warmly, and they seemed to accept that such delays were commonplace in their part of the world. They had kindly set up accommodation, transport, and a meeting venue for us as well.

Edouard and I outlined the programme, showed them a video, and began to discuss the practical requirements and responsibilities of the National Leadership Team that was a requirement for the management of the programme in each country. The response was warm and intelligent. We stressed the unifying effect of the programme upon the church, and there was public agreement and commitment that such a team would consist of as wide a number of denominational representatives as possible. Edouard agreed to return to The Gambia the following month to deliver some more training, and to further establish the process. As challenging as it was to get there, we came away from the meeting fairly confident that the giftbox programme could become a wholesome and helpful offering of the Church to its community.

With such limited time, my exploration of The Gambia was restricted to a relatively short tour of the neighbouring cities of Banjul (the capital) and Serekunda (the largest city). Aside from its access to the Atlantic Ocean, at the mouth of the mighty Gambia River, the country is totally surrounded by Senegal. Its 1.8 million people basically live on a 16km shoreline to the north and south of the Gambia River. Even at its broadest point, the country is less than 50km wide. Sadly, one could say that the key historic reason that The Gambia even existed as a country is the legacy of colonialists, firstly the Portuguese and then the British, who were determined to maintain access to the Gambia River for slave trade purposes. This week, the pastors we had met had lamented the attitude, dress, morals, and work ethic of young Gambians. However, despite regular power cuts and many broken down cars, the country appeared to me to be much cleaner, and the infrastructure better developed than that which I'd seen in Senegal. Peanut export has given way to tourism as the largest income generator, although my visit was in the rainy season, and tourists were few and far between.

On the second of my two mornings in country, I was further restricted by having to stay in my accommodation, due to it being 'eco-Saturday', the one day every month when the only people allowed on the streets were those involved in the cleaning up of the environment. This was a practice I was familiar with in a few former Soviet countries, but this was the first time I had encountered it in Africa. Later I was to discover that Rwanda has a similar requirement and expectation of its citizens.

The Republic of The Gambia is 95% Islamic, although sometimes infused into this are traditional beliefs and practices, such as 'late night calls', rites of passage, animism, female genital mutilation, and the visiting of sacred sites such as crocodile pools, where holy men pray for people's blessing, prosperity and fertility.[1] Although the remaining 5% Christian community lives in relative harmony with its Muslim neighbours, the (Ghanaian and Nigerian) pastors spoke of how their open evangelistic efforts and church services are met with hostility and aggression in certain parts of the country. I wondered if this was, at least in some small part, due to the fact that they were not intrinsic Gambians, and even whether their forthright, almost abrasive approach to evangelism also had some negative impact in this respect.

---

[1] I visited the Kachikaly Crocodile Pool, and a photo of me actually shaking hands with Charley, the largest (and thankfully, most docile) of these creatures can be found on my website, CuttingAcross.com.

The programme we were offering to roll out in The Gambia had huge potential as a bridge builder between the church and the community. When delivered well, it has proved itself to be very relational, and our hosts did seem to understand the value of this. However, the team we spoke with did not appear to include too much integrated social action in the practices of their churches. Impressively, they did provide certain educational services (pre-school and school age education), but apart from that their efforts seemed to be invested more into conventional building-based church activities such as worship and preaching. I was told, for example, that HIV/AIDS is spoken of in the church and to its congregation in terms of the need for abstinence and faithfulness, but they seemed at a loss to tell us about any community-based HIV prevention programmes, which were viewed by some of the pastors that I spoke with as the domain and the responsibility not of the church but of the government.

All this was in contrast to my time with Edouard, who had a much more holistic or integral approach to the Christian gospel. At the time, he had experience of working in at least 24 African countries, translating the bible into many African languages, and working for the Medical Assistance Programme. He also ran his own charity, International Action for Holistic Development (IAHD), which commits to transformational education, social economic development (micro credit, capacity building etc), peace and reconciliation, and health and the environment. Sharing a very similar vision for the ways churches can invest into their communities, we enjoyed some very good and encouraging conversations together.

Having contended with every obstacle to get *to* The Gambia, surely now, with my vast and recently acquired experience of how to negotiate West African transport anomalies, one would think that the return flight would be a doddle. I certainly had hoped so, as I was due to spend just one day and two nights at home before setting off to be the main speaker at a conference on the other side of the globe, in Vancouver, Canada.

The plan was that I would take an evening flight from Banjul back to Dakar, hop on the next flight to Milan, and arrive back in the UK by early the following evening. Unwisely trusting that the planned schedule was fool-proof, I spent the last of my local currency taking a taxi to the airport. Apparently, NASA had invested heavily into the lighting and lengthening of the runway at Banjul International Airport, in order to make it ready for the emergency landing of a space shuttle, should one ever be needed. Granted, I wasn't looking at it from space, but as we approached the airport that evening, I was actually surprised by how dark it was. Normally, at all times of night, a nation's main international airport can be seen for miles, even from space, by the brilliance of its lights. But as we approached the chained gates of the airport in Yundum, 20km south of Banjul, a sleepy guard emerged from a darkened hut, and asked what we were doing there. It transpired that the airline had, once more, cancelled my flight from Banjul. There would be no more flights, in or out of the airport, until tomorrow. Unless of course, a space shuttle got into difficulties. I resigned myself to having already missed the Dakar to Milan flight. With the taillights of the taxi disappearing back down the bumpy road to Banjul, the guard let me through the gates, on the off chance that I could find someone who could help.

Not a soul from the Nigerian-founded, Banjul-based airline Slok Air was to be found. However, on a curled-up leaflet on their abandoned desk I discovered the phone number of their Mr Johnston, who gave me the number of Miss Mariana, who gave me the number of Mr Cooky, Head of Marketing. By the sounds of the loud music and laughter in the background, Mr Cooky was enjoying a raucous party, and was not in the slightest interested in my plight. Or my flight. On a faint, crackling and very expensive phone line, I used all my persuasive charm, or so I thought, to insist that he paid for a taxi back into town, and some overnight accommodation, but at each step he was unwilling to cooperate, or to acknowledge his airline's responsibility. Despite me being so politely British, and a man of peace at that, my voice became stronger and more determined as I told him that if he failed to fulfil his contractual duty, it would become *very* expensive for him to get me to Dakar, then to Milan, then to London, and then to Vancouver by Wednesday.

At this point he admitted his liability to at least get me from Banjul to Dakar. I told him I had no Dalasi (Gambian currency), and he told me to go to Sunrise Hotel in Serekunda, where Slok Air held an account, and where their pilots and cabin crew sometimes stayed. At first, he refused to pay for the room in advance – but eventually I persuaded him to. But he was determined not to pay for a meal for me, nor would he pay for a taxi. Not that there was one.[2]

---

[2] Back in the UK, I discovered that the airline's Air Operators' Certificate had recently been suspended by the Nigerian government, hence them reforming as a Gambian registered airline. I was unsurprised a couple of years later to read of creditors filing lawsuits and seeking payments against the firm, and that despite any formal announcement, press

As I wandered back into the darkened car park, I prayed that some angel would appear, preferably driving a chariot of some sort. A space shuttle would have done, although I guess one requiring an emergency landing wouldn't have been ideal. Two guys were idly chatting together as they leant against their old truck. It was the only vehicle left in the car park. I was glad to be able to tell someone - anyone - my story, so I approached them and introduced myself. I thanked the Lord quietly under my breath as they introduced themselves as from the Church of Pentecost – one of the churches I had met with earlier in the day. Not only did they take me to Sunrise Hotel, but they gave me enough cash to get myself a pizza and a taxi back to the airport the following morning. Late that night, gratefully praising God for my two angels and open backed chariot cum space shuttle, I was nevertheless forced to face the reality of how it had so far taken me six hours to get nowhere, and I still had no idea as to who would fly me home, via where, and by when.

I did make it to Vancouver. I spoke at the conference, and my humble contribution was well received. The purpose of my first visit to West Africa

---

release, or news report, the airline stopped taking bookings, and ceased flying.

had been to host one meeting and, when it eventually happened, it went well. But most memorable for me was the fact that it took me 69 hours to travel there, and a mere 57 hours to get home, via Senegal and Lisbon, as it happened. Living on my own at the time, I recall desperately, dangerously, struggling to *just about* stay awake as I drove the one hundred miles home from Heathrow, of putting the key in the lock of my front door, dragging my case directly to the washing machine, loading it up with my dirty clothes, and continuing to function like a robot in the few hours I had at home, before setting off to the airport once more for the other side of the world.

Swaziland (Eswatini)

During my early years in the employ of Samaritan's Purse, my responsibility was to manage the international distribution of the very popular and high-profile Christmas giftbox programme – Operation Christmas Child. It was my job to ensure that 'National Leadership Teams' were set up and established on good principles in the countries to where the UK sent the gifts - so that approximately one million giftboxes per year were effectively distributed to 'the right child at the right time in the right spirit'.

As with many humanitarian initiatives, the programme came about as a compassionate response to the shock and horror the world felt when made aware of the 'rocking children' in Romanian state orphanages in 1990. It had developed, over a decade and a half, into a humanitarian offering - a simple 'you have not been forgotten' gift - to poor children in many countries, and its partners included NGOs,[3] charities, entrepreneurs, and even governments.

---

[3] Non-Governmental Organisations

I found that in order for it to be true to its purpose and intention, national church leaders and activists were the most intrinsic and appropriate partners to work with, and I sought to steer the programme in this direction. I saw it as a means of them building relationships with the most marginalised in their villages and neighbourhoods as they reached out with a gospel of mercy and kindness. The nations where these gifts were distributed were mainly in the Eastern European regions of the Balkans and former Soviet Union, but I also made visits to the African nations of Mozambique, The Gambia, and Swaziland for this same purpose.

For my first visit to the Kingdom of Swaziland, I had hired a car and travelled overland from Maputu, the capital of neighbouring Mozambique where I had been visiting, and where the programme was already in full swing.

I had been tasked to find suitable partners in Swaziland so that the giftbox programme could also commence there. On my first day in the country, and through the friend of a colleague, I managed to meet with the Executive Committee of the Swaziland Conference of Churches, a dignified group of men who represented all the mainstream churches across the country. I gave them a brief outline of the principles, purposes, and practices of the giftbox programme, and answered a few of their questions. What I was suggesting was met with considerable, palpable interest and enthusiasm by the meeting and with the full endorsement of their president who, with a big and commanding smile, leaned back in his chair and loudly declared, "Permission is Granted", at which the meeting broke into spontaneous applause.

Out of that meeting a team was formed that over the coming years would prove to be an excellent, dynamic team which frequently 'went the extra mile', and became a model of good practice for the giftbox programme. But the focus of my role within Samaritan's Purse was soon to change, and it would be almost a decade before I returned to Swaziland.

In total, I made four visits to Swaziland. Five, if you include returning from a two day hop across the border to South Africa. In 2018, to celebrate the King's birthday, this tiny nation changed its name to Eswatini, or eSwatini. Swaziland, Eswatini, eSwatini. Any which way, they all mean 'the land of the Swazis'. As my visits there were all made just before the name change, in this chapter I will refer to it as Swaziland.

Squeezed in between Mozambique and South Africa, and with a population of around one million, landlocked Swaziland is Africa's only absolute monarchy, a term also used to describe the autocracy that royals still maintain in other countries such as Brunei, Oman, Saudi Arabia, Vatican City, and each of the United Arab Emirates. Although the world's longest reigning monarch is often thought to be Queen Elizabeth II, King Sobhuza II actually reigned in Swaziland for just short of 83 years, until his death in 1982. The present King Mswati III was crowned in 1986. Reigning over a poor country (which also regularly has the dubious distinction of having the highest percentage of HIV/AIDS cases in the world), the King has been fiercely criticised in the media for his lavish lifestyle, to say nothing of his having fifteen wives and several concubines. I found that those I spoke with were always extremely respectful of their King, or *Ngwenyama*, and of their traditions and their very different culture. However, although the nation always presented itself to me, a mere visitor, as relatively peaceful, it was clear from media reports that many of its citizens were strongly advocating for constitutional reforms. In the twelve years between my first and most recent visits to Swaziland, a number of pro-democracy protests intermittently broke out, often sparking riots, looting and street skirmishes with soldiers and police.

On the first of my visits, I recall sitting in my hired car, waiting at red traffic lights in Manzini city centre. Streams of pedestrians crossed the road in front of me, and I realised that wherever I looked, every person was younger than my own sons. It was the beginning of my comprehension as to what a nation looked like when four out of every ten people are living (or dying) with HIV.

When I arrived for my next visit eight years later, my luggage didn't, requiring a hasty visit to a shopping mall for some essentials. I stayed at Mountain Inn which, despite being only 3km from the capital city, commands wonderful views over the Ewulwini Valley – 'the Valley of Heaven'. Talking of heaven, upon my arrival someone had quite incidentally mentioned to me that the lodge was run by Christians, a fact that was confirmed to me as I entered the breakfast room the following morning.

Background music gently soothed the spirits of the small handful of diners. The song being played was very familiar to me. By now a global hit with worship bands in churches throughout the world, it had been written twenty-five years previously by my colleague, Stuart Garrard, who had headed up our music ministry when I was pastor of Praise Community Church in Kettering, UK. I recalled how Stuart had wandered through to my office one day, guitar strap around his neck, strumming his latest tune and saying, "What do you think of this one?" As someone who needs to hear a song two or three times before having an opinion on it, I remember how, unintentionally, I had damned him with my faint praise. "It's all right, I suppose." Having been the first person in the world to hear that song, here I was, being serenaded by it once more as I ate my breakfast in a tiny and relatively unknown nation in the Southern Hemisphere.

Following that visit, I worked closely with our Raising Families partnership team in Swaziland. Their director, Wandy, and I would travel long miles, working together not only in Swaziland but also in the UK and in South Africa. Our conversations were always stimulating and mutually encouraging. Wandy felt passionately that Africa did not need Western handouts and sympathy, but that God had given it all the resources it needed to succeed. Supported by my employers, he and his team led highly effective community development programmes which greatly empowered local families, churches and communities, particularly related to livelihood and water and sanitation initiatives. Like many of our partners across the continent, Wandy loved and believed in God, and looked to Him for his needs.

One sad day, when I told him it looked likely that Samaritan's Purse would no longer be able to fund his work, he smiled. "It's not a vision of faith unless it's unachievable," he said. "That's how God works. Why do you need God when you can manage a process yourself? He has wired us for impossibilities. The bible is full of that."

I spent many days talking through these programmes with him, monitoring their progress and meeting people from some of the 560 churches and 11,000 families he was working with in rural communities all over the country. We were consistently welcomed with song, dance, drama and food. I was given ceremonial cloaks, bracelets, neck-beads and live chickens. I heard story after story of lives and communities transformed, despite the enormous setbacks they had encountered through long term drought and the practices of some large commercial farming cooperatives and absentee landlords, who would heartlessly use their power and influence to grab disproportionate amounts of water for their own land, leaving their poor subsistence farmer neighbours with none.

The communities we visited would often set up stalls (similar to those one could expect to find in a UK village hall craft fare), and exhibit their products as a visual reflection of the businesses they had started. At one place there were items of homemade clothing, oils, jams, honey, lemon grass, live fish and chickens, and soaps. At the next there were building blocks, catapults, plants, wooden and metal furniture, polishes, jewellery, cushions, mats and brooms. Our hosts would invite us to sit with people from their savings-and-loans clubs, and insist that I took a very detailed look at their paperwork, so as to vouch for their accuracy, integrity and accountability. Or I would be taken to see their field crops, their livestock, or their community bore hole. These were communities that had previously shared their water sources with cattle, donkeys, dogs, frogs and bats. Instances of cholera in their villages were not unknown. I would listen to formal speeches from community leaders, and heart-felt, tear-filled stories of gratitude from the most marginalised in their neighbourhoods. Rural church leaders told me of the extensive literacy and bible training programme that they had completed, and I heard about the amazing graduation ceremonies that were held to celebrate their completion. Such events were clearly the highlight of many of these pastors' lives.

Wanting us to see the fruit of their labour and to celebrate with them, some communities and programme participants would hold back the harvesting of their crops until the day we visited. One such farm was worked by several ageing ladies. We 'helped' them to harvest cayenne peppers (which are apparently good for treating TB and other sicknesses), drought resistant jalapeno and habanero peppers, and moringa trees. Their garden plots were totally organic. They used cow and chicken manure, vegetable mulch, non-chemical insecticides and grew plants that alkaline the soil.

"Because the pump has broken down, we are only limited by how many water vessels we can carry on our heads up from the dam," the team leader told us, with vessel-half-full positivity in her voice. "We also have a thriving savings-and-loans scheme," she added. And then, without any hint of irony in this drought-parched landscape she concluded, "We're saving for a rainy day".[4]

We would try to cram in visits to four or five different communities in a day, and invariably our estimates of when we would arrive at each location got further and further set back as the day progressed. It was incredibly difficult to tear ourselves away from each place and, painfully, we sometimes had to decline the meals that they had been lovingly preparing for us for hours. Patient hosts would walk from dawn to come to the meeting point (often a church hall or

---

[4] Many more of these testimonies feature in my book, 'Raising Families: Envisioning the Church to Empower its Neighbourhood'. ISBN: 978-1-0914-1053-4

community centre, or maybe under a particular tree), wait for hours for our late arrival, and spend some time with us, maybe another hour, before walking many miles in the dark to get home again. Witnessing their appreciation, and understanding their devotion certainly put my long days into perspective.

Here are my notes from one such day:

I didn't sleep well last night, firstly due to the thunder and lightning at midnight, followed by the lashing rain on the tin roof until 3am, and then the howling gale-force wind which I thought would blow the roof off at 5am.

The weather calmed down and was dry but still with stormy clouds as Wandy and I drove south-east to Sithobela, which took an hour on tarmac and another hour on dirt roads. I had been asked to dress much smarter than usual with a shirt, tie and jacket, as I was billed as the 'keynote speaker' at one of the pastors' and CAG[5] leaders' graduations. It was the fourth such event that BBI has held this year. Crowded into a big public hall cum indoor market, and representing about 77 churches were 270 people, some of whom had travelled a considerable

---

[5] Church Action Groups

journey to get there. All the graduates wore long black gowns and a square, black, mortarboard hat, hired for the occasion. At least four or five of the BBI[6] coordinators were there, some like Gugu and Samgelo whom I'd met before, but it was a very dark room which depended on a small generator for a little light and sound, this morning's storm having blown out the mains electric supply before we arrived, causing the whole programme to be set back an hour.

Tinkhundla leaders, archbishops and bishops were all there, seated at the front of the hall with me and Wandy and some of the BBI guys. Among the graduates was one *Tinkhundla* leader and one future leader, the headmaster of a school, and several other people with important responsibilities in the community. The event was excellently conducted by a young MC. There was worship, speeches, introductions and talks, and one by one those who preceded me spoke almost exactly on what I had planned in my head to say in my much publicised (and by my reckoning, over-egged) 'keynote' speech.

Speakers didn't only congratulate, comfort and encourage. They were motivational, urgent in their instruction to the graduates to press on further.

---

[6] Bridge Builders International

Samgelo spoke very powerfully about God's intention for us to work hard, and that the lazy man should not eat.

"Take care of what He has given you," he urged the crowd. "Maximise what God has put in your hand. When people complain that chickens eat their crops, I say, 'Where were you? Take care of your crops and work hard!' Read Proverbs 24:30, and 28:19!"[7]

I sat in my seat, determinedly resisting the temptation of being overburdened with the word 'keynote'. I had been in this sort of spotlight many times before. Yet again this morning, it was a case of 'don't get ready; be ready', and it wasn't until I took a deep breath and stood to my feet that I finally decided the content of my talk.

---

[7] Proverbs 24:30-34 says:

[30] I went past the field of a sluggard, past the vineyard of someone who has no sense;
[31] thorns had come up everywhere, the ground was covered with weeds, and the stone wall was in ruins.
[32] I applied my heart to what I observed and learned a lesson from what I saw:
[33] A little sleep, a little slumber, a little folding of the hands to rest—
[34] and poverty will come on you like a thief and scarcity like an armed man.

And Proverbs 28:19 says:

[19] Those who work their land will have abundant food, but those who chase fantasies will have their fill of poverty.

I then had the privilege of shaking the hand of every graduate, and giving them their certificate. Whilst posing with each one for a photo, I sought to speak blessing and protection upon them. I was then given gifts of shirts, a tablecloth, a bowl, two envelopes, and a purse for Mr Alan and some beads for Mrs Alan. It wasn't until I arrived home to the UK that I realised that the two envelopes actually had cash in them as a gift to me and Bela, totalling 100 Lilangeni, or about £5.50.

Amazingly all the guests were then given a substantial cooked meal and drink. After which came the time for more photos. Just as all the graduates stepped out of the door, the heavens opened once more, and we spent a chaotic 30 minutes trying to take photos back in the indoor gloom. Just before Wandy and I left, at about 3pm, the rain stopped and we managed to take some photos outside, but disappointingly it wasn't of the whole group. But what an occasion, and what a privilege.

It's not cannibals, elephants, terrorists or even mosquitos that end the lives of most missionaries and aid workers in 'the field', but car accidents. I am so very grateful for God's protection during all my many road journeys around the world. Despite travelling in some very suspect vehicles and on some terrible roads where potholes gape, goats wander and children play, and being driven by drivers who have no sense of fear and have been awake for more than 24 hours, I have never been involved in a road accident overseas. Almost, but not quite.

Leaving one of these rural Swazi communities, we drove in convoy down the dirt road leading back to the main highway. We were already behind schedule and were aware that other groups were waiting for our arrival. I was travelling with Wandy, and behind us was his colleague Tananile, in an old RAV4. Turning a bend, she lost control of the car and it rolled over onto its roof, crashed through the undergrowth and into a ditch by the side of the road. Wandy saw it all happen in his rear-view mirror and the first I knew of it was him braking hard and exclaiming, "Tananile, what on earth are you *doing*!?"

She was trapped upside down in the car for a short while as we worked out how to open the doors, all of which had been bashed well out of shape by the impact. After a few minutes, Tananile managed to crawl out of the front passenger door through the broken glass, seriously shaken but seemingly able to walk. We helped her back to Wandy's car. She had bashed her leg and her neck hurt, but otherwise was in one piece. When a larger four-wheel drive vehicle came along, the driver kindly offered to tow the RAV4 back onto its now twisted wheels and dragged it into the side of the road. There was no doubt that the vehicle was a 'write off' and Wandy had to make several calls to the police and insurance officials before we could leave the site and get Tananile to the hospital. Later we heard she was fine, and was discharged without serious injury. But this was yet another day when a community had to patiently wait several hours for our arrival.

Liberia

The immigration office at Roberts International Airport, an hour's drive east of Monrovia, is probably the most chaotic I've encountered anywhere in the world. Not unfriendly. Just totally disorganised. It would have been entirely possible to walk right through the mayhem and out of the airport without reference to anyone. However, without an entry stamp in one's passport one is regarded as having entered a country illegally and risks a hefty fine, or worse, upon departure. I once spent a wonderful week in one former Soviet Union country on this somewhat precarious basis, but that's another story.

But here, on my first and, so far, only visit to Liberia, I had to abandon my noble British instinct to queue, and pushed and shoved my way to an old table, behind which stood several young immigration officers. Collectively, they looked more like a boyband than the formal guardians of their sovereign borders. Hopping, almost dancing, from foot to foot, each one of them cheerily engaged in a continual stream of banter and laughter as they worked haphazardly through the passport documents of the latest arrivals. Liberia has virtually no tourists.

Those who do come tend to be here for purposes of business, politics, mission, or family visits. As I thrust my passport into the hand of one of the officers, I anticipated a couple of questions as to why I'd come. But the interview took an unexpected turn.

He called to his colleagues. "Here guys, have a look at this one!"

"Oh no," I thought, "I have a previous passport entry for a country that Liberia regards as a sworn enemy, and they won't let me in." I have two passports, partly for this reason, but hadn't thought this was an issue in Liberia.

And it wasn't. Upon opening my passport to the front page, the officer who had condescended to inspect it had merely become intrigued with my place of birth, which is a small market town in the north of Suffolk.

"Hey guys! This Alan Cutting was born in Eye!" Abandoning my other exasperated travelling companions, several of the officers crowded round to stare at my passport, then at me, and then back at my passport. Then they pointed at me and cracked up with uncontrollable laughter.

"No way! Honestly? Is that a real place?" one asked with incredulity. Not having had much of a say as to the place in which I was born, or indeed the naming of said place, I was forced into a situation I know all too well. It is that crossroads between extroversion and introversion, between confidence and shyness. Do I join in with the banter, or just shrivel up and die a slow, painful, and embarrassing death in response to what was, in essence, officialdom?

"Yes," I said, with a half-hearted attempt at appearing confident enough to enter into the joke. "I was born in Eye, and my parents are buried in Bury." It's true. But they clearly thought Eye was funnier than I. Or should that be 'me'?

Dwelling with resentment on the fact that England must have the silliest place names in the world, I left the airport, found a taxi, and immediately drove through the town of … Smell-no-Taste. The story goes that this settlement grew up around a base for American GI's, inaccessible to the locals, and the delicious aromas of their cooking wafted across the town. I started to feel a little better about the name of the town in which I was born.

In fact, during that trip I was reliably informed that Liberia has a colourful array of place names, including Buzzi Quarters, Toe Town, Fish Town, Underwears Town, Boo Town, Bong County and Plonker. But it wasn't until doing some family research a number of years later that I discovered that its capital, Monrovia, was named after one of my very own relatives, US President James Munro. Well, when I say 'relative', I don't exactly mean brother, cousin, or even father-in-law. In fact, the blood runs so thin that I have reduced the detail, in all its obscurity, to a footnote.[8]

So, what was the reason for my visit, the reason that the immigration officials found so much less interesting than the place of my birth? A few years later, I would be sending doctors and nurses into front line, pioneering roles in Liberia, in the fight against Ebola. From my UK base, I would be liaising with Public Health England and Public Health Wales towards the creation of new policies and practices for these heroic medics' safe repatriation. Due to her experiences in Liberia, one of these doctors would become a global expert on Ebola and other infectious diseases and would be regularly called on by BBC and Channel 4 News to be a spokesperson on current issues surrounding Ebola, Covid etc.

---

[8] My great grandfather's brother, Aubrey Cutting, immigrated to Colorado in the 1880s. Aubrey's son, George, married one Helen Robinson. Helen's paternal grandmother, Francis Robinson, nee Monroe, was grandniece to President James Monroe (1758-1831), fifth President of the United States, and final President to be a Founding Father of the United States. As if this shameless name-dropping was not enough, Helen's father, Theodore Douglas Robinson was a nephew of President Theodore Roosevelt, and her mother's father, James 'Rosy' Roosevelt (1854-1927) was President Franklin D Roosevelt's half-brother. Have a nice day.

But on this visit, I had come to Liberia for an entirely different purpose. I was here to join a team of ex-professional and semi-professional footballers and coaches, who regularly travelled with my organisation to various countries in order to offer football coaching to marginalised children. In a world where aid is usually offered from an adult to an adult, this was an initiative that focused on the child itself, thereby giving them dignity and a chance to play in proper, sometimes national stadiums. It was an amazing programme, which attracted sponsorship from Liverpool, Manchester United and Newcastle United football clubs, in the form of kit and equipment donations, and I'm sure boys and girls all over the world will long remember those special days when they were trained and played at their own 'Wembley' equivalent.

But it was a massively expensive programme to deliver, and my bosses back home were asking increasingly difficult questions about its sustainability. Lacking much evidence of delivering long term change, it was seen as being at risk of becoming an exclusive and exotic club for those chosen to travel on the teams. What's more, the highly charismatic founder and leader of the soccer programme was about to leave the organisation. Having recently taken over the short-term mission team programme, I was asked to go to Liberia in order to see how this model worked in Africa. Then, just before I left home, my seniors made the decision that they could no longer justify the expense of this programme. I was therefore given the unenviable task of explaining to the team leader and its members why this would be their final such trip.

By the time I arrived, late on a Sunday evening in November, the team had been there for three days, each day being spent coaching children at the ATS stadium in Monrovia. I joined them the next morning for a visit to THINK girl's home in Monrovia, before we undertook what was the team's first trip out of the capital.

Gbarnga is the capital of Bong County, three hours north-east of Monrovia. Ma Feata had invited us to stay with her and the children at her Rainbow Town orphanage for two days, the second of which was spent coaching 450 children in the local stadium.

Liberia's fourteen years of war (1989-2003) had wrecked so much of the country's social fabric. More than 300,000 are said to have died in war-related deaths, whole communities were displaced, and children were recruited as soldiers. There were ten registered orphanages at the start of the first conflict. Two years later there were 121.

The summary conclusion of the Human Rights in Liberia's Orphanages report, published by United Nations four months after my visit, looked into the general state of Liberian orphanages. It soberly concluded that

> Children living in Liberian orphanages are denied their fundamental rights on a daily basis. They live in conditions that are substandard, do not receive adequate health care, and are given few educational and developmental opportunities. The experiences of a child growing up in an orphanage are likely to have effects that will last into adulthood, and therefore impact society as a whole.[9]

Happily, the report specifically praised Rainbow Town orphanage, our hosts, as a model of good practice, citing it as one of only a handful where each child had a mattress on which to sleep. In the vast majority of the orphanages monitored by the report, three children, and in one case seven, would share one mattress.

During the week before Christmas, 1989, the world was simultaneously experiencing several extraordinary political earthquakes. All European

---

[9] https://www.refworld.org/pdfid/473daddb0.pdf

eyes were focused on Romania, and the complete collapse of the Ceaușescu regime, triggering off the rapid disintegration of the Iron Curtain. Meanwhile, on the other side of the pond George H. W. Bush's US was invading Panama, seeking to depose their de facto leader, Manuel Noriega.[10] But Romania and Panama were the last things on the minds of Liberians, as that was also the week when Charles Taylor and his National Patriotic Front of Liberia took up arms against the Liberian government. After being unable to capture the nation's capital, Gbarnga became the base for the rebel group that initiated the first Liberian civil war.

Gbarnga is also the home of the Cuttington University, the oldest private, coeducational, four-year, degree-granting institution in sub-Saharan Africa. I was intrigued to discover that it is named after its original benefactor, one Robert Fulton Cutting. In 1887, he donated $5,000 to an Episcopalian bishop in Liberia for the establishment of a school for teaching Liberian children, regardless of ethnicity, about industry and agriculture. My namesake was a New York financier and

---

[10] That week I was in Managua, capital of Sandinista-led Nicaragua, and the word on the street, inaccurately as it turned out, was that Panama's Manuel Noriega had fled to the city for refuge. I recall keeping my head down as truckloads of hostile young teenagers armed with AK47s toured the streets, and I witnessed one young man being shot in the foot for deserting from the army. Dangerous and exciting times.

philanthropist, who is also credited with starting the sugar beet industry in the United States in 1888, and of laying out the country's first private golf course in 1895.

We had one more location in which to deliver the football programme. This was in the Doris Williams Stadium in Buchanan, three hours south of Monrovia. The Doris Williams Stadium is the home of Mighty Barrole FC, the club where George Weah, Liberia's most famous footballer and now the country's president, began his career. That day, 350 children joined the programme, including some girls - former child soldiers - from a local orphanage. "Getting these children to play," we were told by our host, "is a significant part of their rehabilitation."

The team travelled in two large minibuses, and few had encountered a journey like it. We bumped and slid our way through roads pitted with enormous potholes. One was so deep that for a second or two we in the second vehicle quite literally lost sight of the leading minibus. This 'African massage' was quite a challenge for footballers used to very much more refined methods of travel and, for some, it was sadly not a change embraced with very good grace.

But overall, the team of footballers was great fun, and they worked hard. There was a tremendous sense of camaraderie and hilarity about almost everything they did. Their strong banter was usually built around three or four dominant and loud personalities. Breaking into this tight and vibrant unit on day four, not being a footballer, and coming as I did with news of the programme's end wasn't the easiest gig but, on the whole, I was warmly received by the team. It was the sort of environment where everyone was teased constantly, and although I think the victims accepted it without offence, one shouldn't be too sensitive on this sort of trip, or would get thoroughly crushed somewhere along the line. My training on standing up for myself in the face of collective and public ridicule, so recently undertaken at airport immigration, stood me in good stead.

Uganda

The Ugandan Primate pointed at me authoritatively, almost aggressively, as we drove into central London. "Alan! You *will* protect me from the British press!"

It was, most definitely, more of a command than a request. I was hosting the visit to the UK of two African Anglican Archbishops, those of Rwanda and Uganda. They had agreed together to come to the UK for seven days, to speak at conferences and churches on the very positive impact of Raising Families, the Church and Community Development programme that I managed in their countries. Not only was I their host, but also their driver, their fixer and, it now seemed to me, their bodyguard and protector from the press. I had left home that morning at 3 o'clock, had picked them up at Heathrow from their overnight flight from Nairobi, and was now driving them to Lambeth Palace for their breakfast appointment with the Archbishop of Canterbury.

Despite his influence, I always found His Grace, the Archbishop of Rwanda (now retired) to be a wonderfully wise and peaceful man, full of grace and humility, and he was good company as we travelled around the country. He had become a personal friend and had for a number of years been of enormous help to me, by motivating the 1,400 churches in his care to engage fully with the Raising Families programme. He also wrote a warm endorsement for my first book, 'Cutting Across the Borders'.

But I had only met His Grace, the then Archbishop of Uganda (also now retired), once before. His personality and his leadership style were, shall we say, rather more assertive. He was big and bold. "Basically, my job description is to be the pastor of 35 million people," he told me.

This was his second visit to the UK in two weeks. On the previous visit, he had caused a stir across the media by walking out of a major Primates Meeting in Canterbury over a highly contentious theological and political issue. He had not enjoyed the subsequent treatment of the British press and, despite now being with me in the UK to maximise publicity for my programme, he was insistent that I should protect him from our nation's journalists. This could be a challenge, I thought to myself. But I felt very honoured that these two men had been willing to come all that way to spend time with me. And despite one more altercation later that same morning (an all too loud clash with an obnoxious retired vicar in the quiet sophistication of the prestigious Athenaeum Club in Pall Mall!), thankfully the week settled into a pattern that was, on the whole, both enjoyable and constructive.

I worked with 480 of the Archbishop's Anglican churches in Uganda, in the two diocese of Masindi-Kitara and West Lango, and collectively these churches committed to working with 9,600 of the poorest families in their neighbourhoods. We envisioned and equipped them to walk with the ultra-poor as they climbed out of their poverty - spiritually, practically, emotionally, relationally, and societally.[11] But of all the Raising Families programmes I managed around the world, the Ugandan one was probably the most challenging. Being a programme that sought to envision and mobilise local churches, families, and communities to come together and use what they already had, in order that they might experience genuine transformation in their neighbourhoods, an essential ingredient was that of developing a good community work ethic.

---

[11] Many of their stories are featured in my book 'Raising Families - Envisioning the Church to Empower its Neighbourhood'. ISBN 978-1-0914-1053-4

However, over the previous decade or two, these regions of Uganda had been particularly hard hit by conflict and famine. As a result, many international NGOs had poured into the region, almost all of which offered free aid and resources, or 'hand-outs'. So much so - and in some cases so indiscriminately - that the work ethic of the local population was being severely damaged. Over a period of time and in too many cases, aid had been given without intelligent thought about how to turn this into a strategy for development, and consequently a dependency culture was becoming more and more deeply engrained in local people's thinking. Already contending with some very tough and challenging circumstances, these communities were now learning a very negative, poverty-based worldview which would do nothing to equip them to flourish in the longer term. Local men and women were even offered what were called 'sitting fees', i.e. payments given as a reward to those who merely attended certain trainings offered by some of these NGOs.

These communities had already heard a lot about Samaritan's Purse which, being a conventional international NGO, often undertook programmes that were based on giving resources, such as food, tools, water filters, wells etc. Given that background, my task (which was to envision communities to recognise, rise up and use their *own* resources) was challenging. The relationships I sought to build often started shakily, with responses including extreme lethargy and negativity, ultra-cautiousness, mistrust and, on some occasions, open and collective hostility. It was not only the families and communities who could not see past the provision of hand-outs, but even some of the Anglican clergy, including the bishop.

I worked through a very patient and capable team (national employees of Samaritan's Purse), but even some of them had learned this one-way aid approach, and had moments when they doubted the vision and felt they could not carry on. I had to be ruthlessly honest with myself, and look deeply into the culture and mindset of those I was working with and those we were seeking to serve, and to pit all that resistance against the vision for self-sustainability that I so deeply believed in. At times I felt that mine was a lone and sometimes even cruel voice, and that I was trying to cut against a deeply established grain. If I had not seen it work so well in other similar African environments (particularly in Swaziland, Rwanda, and Zambia), I think the Ugandans might have convinced me that this method of community development could not work. But we stuck with it, and on each successive visit I found an increasing understanding and appreciation of, confidence in, and commitment to the Raising Families process.

On my most recent visit to his office, one senior project manager at Samaritan's Purse humbly recalled his cynicism in the early days of the programme, when he quite strongly felt that capital investment would be needed to see any significant change. I remember some difficult conversations with him about this, and also about our training manuals, which he had said were too simplistic and idealistic, and just not practical or detailed enough.

"To be honest, when I visited some of the Church Action Groups recently, I was very impressed with just how much can be done without injection of funds," he confessed. "I was very surprised - I've never seen it before where people not only help themselves but help others. I particularly loved the ingenuity of some people. One guy took a loan and now recycles garbage, and he testifies as to how much the training has helped him."

On the same visit, the Bishop of Masindi told me how he had also become convinced, albeit by the impact on his churches. "One (Raising Families) Church Action Group leader is better than ten pastors! Our churches are becoming full now, and there's greatly improved unity between the denominations."

So encouraged was he that he began to sing the praises of Raising Families with his national colleagues. It was him who persuaded his Archbishop to come to the UK to testify of its impact and thereby seek to generate more awareness and funds for it.

I wrote about my first visit to Uganda, which had taken place a handful of years earlier, in the introductory chapter of my book, Cutting Across the Borders. It included the story of a quite miraculous evening that reaffirmed to me a childhood dream I had had, of travelling the world to speak of the gospel. I have taken the liberty of including it again in this chapter.

> Having clearly become a Christian when I was eight years old, it wasn't very long - probably a year or two - before I began to daydream repeatedly about travelling to far-away lands and telling people about Jesus. The dream always involved me speaking from a stage, or a platform. I would have this dream so regularly that the images, even the details, became well established in my mind's eye. Then my unassuming reason would come guiltily to its senses, and I would apologise. "I'm sorry, Lord," I would say. "I'm dreaming

dreams that are far too big for me. I'm just your servant." And with that I would bashfully push away the dream, until it would stir up inside me on another day.

In recent years I have told this story to people in many nations and cultures all over the world, and I conclude by telling my audience that, in His mercy, God actually responded to the *dream* rather than to the apology.

In 2009 I told this story in Atiak, a small rural town in Northern Uganda. I was leading a team of UK volunteers that had journeyed there to learn about the water and sanitation programmes that were supported by my employer, Samaritan's Purse. We visited the Connect Africa Resource Centres (CARC) in Northern Uganda, one of which is situated in the mainly Acholi village of Atiak, just twenty kilometres south of the South Sudanese border. Atiak is a small town made world famous by two massacres, one in 1995 and another a decade later, when the LRA[12] attacked and killed an unknown number of its adults and children. Local people told us,

---

[12] Lord's Resistance Army

"They showed no mercy. They torched our houses, raped and butchered." We heard stories of how children had been rounded up and forced to eat the chopped up remains of their headmaster, before being killed, and the parents told that if they took the bodies for burial, they too would be murdered. Consequently, the rotting remains of their children lay down the road at the school for months.

Ours was a team of twelve. The ten guys slept on bunks in one room, the two women were in a separate room, and many of the locals slept in other corners of the primitive CARC centre. Though the shooting stars were magnificent, they didn't light the path to the eco-san toilets, which were quite a trek away at the back of the centre.

Connect Africa work through the local pastors and churches to encourage a holistic style of ministry (or service) into each community in which they have a presence. Simple clean water and sanitation technology are as much a part of their Christian witness as preaching, teaching, and healing the sick. All these aspects of the Kingdom of God nestle comfortably alongside one another in their work, without conflict or debate.

So that night, Wednesday 17 June 2009, as part of their offering to the village, Connect Africa hosted one of their occasional three-night festivals on the town's tufted football pitch, bordered not by terracing, floodlights or changing rooms but by tiny round huts made of straw roofs and cow-dung walls – the dwelling place of thousands of Internally Displaced People.

An area the size of a five-a-side pitch was roped off in front of the stage, which unfolded out of an old truck – PA, speakers, lights and all. The local believers were invited inside the ropes, where they spent two hours worshipping, dancing and, let's be honest, gathering a crowd. That night the crowd attracted by their worship reportedly numbered around 3,000. Unexpectedly, it was then that the CARC director quite casually asked us foreigners to lead the evening's festivities - just because we were there.

My team looked at me wide-eyed. Just before leaving the UK, one by one, they had talked openly and vulnerably with one another about the heavy blow's life had recently dealt them.

They had shared about how tender they were feeling at this particular time in their lives, even to the point of being unsure as to whether they should come on the trip or not. They had confessed how much they lacked confidence, even over the relatively simple practical task of the team which was, ostensibly, merely to observe the water and sanitation programmes to which Samaritan's Purse was committed in Uganda. And here I was, giving them about 15 minutes' preparation to lead a whole evening of power evangelism in front of an audience of 3,000 traumatised people, not one of whom spoke English.

Carl had a guitar (which he had brought on the trip for team devotionals) and I knew that Tom used to preach.

"Well, guys," I asked, "are you up for it?" Carl was happy to lead worship, but Tom said no to preaching.

"I'm sorry, mate," he said with the strain of defeat all over his face. "You know I used to do that sort of thing but, since my wife was unfaithful and left me, life has fallen apart for me. I left all that sort of ministry thing behind years ago. That's why I've just got my head down making money these days. Sorry mate, but I just can't help you tonight."

Now I'm not a pushy guy, and 99% of the time I would have accepted that answer without question. And yet that evening something prompted me to ask again. Again, Tom said no. So I said, "OK Tom, no worries. But after Carl has done his stuff, I'm going to tell a story, and then I'm going to turn to you where you're standing in the shadows on the edge of the stage, and I'll simply ask you: 'Tom, yes; or Tom, no?' If you say yes, the stage is yours. If you say no, I carry on preaching, and no one will have any idea what that snippet of conversation was about."

In response, Tom just had the time to shrug his shoulders at me and, with interpreter in tow, we were hustled into position. It was time to start.

So I got Carl to belt out some songs – 'Greatest Day in History/O Happy Day' (huge cheer) - we told our audience where we were from (Liverpool, Manchester; two more huge cheers and big stirring of intrigue in the crowd), and then I told them all a story.

What was the story I told to these 3,000 impossibly pained people of Atiak that evening? Well, as the crowd spilled out of their little mud and straw huts, and pressed in to cover the length and breadth of the football pitch and beyond, and a stormy darkness fell over yet another day of abject and lethargic poverty, with all my heart I wanted this unbelievably battered community to dare to dream dreams again. So I simply told them the story of my guilt-ridden and repeated childhood dream - the one about me crossing cultures and standing on a stage to share the love of Jesus with crowds of people - and of how as a lad I kept repenting, and of how God had heard the *dream*, not the apology.

And as I testified, and as I looked down onto that frail portable stage and out into the swollen crowd, slowly an incredible, spine-shivering realisation dawned on me. I'd been here before! It was *here*! This was it; this was absolutely it. This *was* the stage. This was the crowd. This was the setting. This was the event. This was the very place I used to see in my dreams in 1963! I had actually seen Atiak, Northern Uganda, and this rickety little platform, 46 years previously. Amazing.

But I had no time to get too emotional about this extraordinary and supernatural revelation. After all, there were 3,000 people staring at me and waiting for the rest of the meeting. So, finishing my story, I turned my gaze to the edge of the stage and, in a quiet voice simply asked, "Tom, yes; or Tom, no?"

"Yes!" said Tom, and jumped forward to take the microphone from me. Loving nothing better than to help equip and restore people, especially those who have felt defeated by disappointments, I was *delighted*. And do you know what? I don't think I have *ever* heard anyone preach as powerfully as Tom did that night in Atiak. Hundreds of people asked to receive Christ that evening. Many were healed, and delivered from ugly demons that manifest themselves through the writhing of bodies on the ground.

My team, the vast majority of whom had never previously witnessed demonic manifestations or been involved in deliverance (certainly not in the way they were happening that night), just had to get on with it. Whatever conclusions their carefully analysed theological viewpoints might have led them to believe up till that point in their lives, they knew that there, writhing and screaming before them, was a massive spiritual need and, right there and then, it was going to have to be Jesus or bust.

The training I gave my team on deliverance ministry that night was restricted to one-line instructions yelled into team members' ears over the commotion as they laid hands on people and prayed. So ugly was the manifestation of one of the demons that one team member physically took a large step backwards in shock, almost landing on my foot. I pushed him forward again, shouting to him above the din, "Ian, if ever you believed in the Name of Jesus, then believe in it now!" And in he went again for more.

It was an open heaven. Quite extraordinary!

After the main event, the evening was scheduled to end quite late with a showing of The Jesus Film. (We were told that sometimes in this setting whole families would stay on till four in the morning watching film after film.) That night a huge rainstorm ended the film show early, and the track back to the CARC centre with its eco-san toilet was paved with puddles. I walked home slowly with Tom, a small torch guiding our way through the pitch black to the concrete floor which was to be our bed for the night. We were almost silent. I remember saying only one thing.

"Tom; well done mate. That took a different sort of faith than you needed for the preaching you used to do when you were young, didn't it?"

Tom didn't say a word - just shrugged once more, and nodded in almost rueful agreement. He knew exactly what I meant. And another man was on the road to restoration.

The following morning an extraordinarily vivid rainbow arced over the horizon, its ends pressed down into fields of sodden maize. It surrounded us; it dwarfed us; it mesmerised us. It seemed that this particular rainbow just would not fade. We packed our vehicle and left the village and, as the bus carefully dipped and splashed its way through deep red puddles of African mud, I stared quietly out of the window. How did the miraculous events of last night actually happen? My repeated boyhood dream had, quite literally and specifically, been played out before my eyes, with 3,000 people looking on. Why now?

Why here? Yet again I was forced to reflect on the overwhelming faithfulness and spectacular promises of God and how, despite my limited abilities, my questionable confidence and the sheer harmlessness and normality of my life, He had steered me to so many amazing places, introduced me to such extraordinary people, and done such magnificent things for me. Whatever the boundaries, borders and limits I had set up for myself, God had pushed me through them all.[13]

On that same visit to Northern Uganda, one of our more bizarre experiences was that of meeting the Chief of Police in the village of Opit. After a day of travel, Opit was to be our home for the night. On arrival, we were introduced to the local pastors and, for reasons unknown, had a special guest appearance from the Chief Inspector of Police. After the pastors had introduced themselves, it was the turn of the Chief Inspector to speak. I'm very regularly in meetings where local dignitaries are invited to speak and welcome us to their communities, but I have never before heard a Police Chief introduce himself in the way the Chief Inspector of Opit did. He shouted,

---

[13] Cutting Across the Borders, p 6-11. ISBN: 978-1-7200-2050-9. And the rainbow I describe here is the cover picture of this book.

"Praise the Lord! Praise the Lord! Hallelujah!" And then he told us his story.

He had been arrested by the LRA, then escaped and fled into the jungle for two years. During this time, assuming he was dead, his family held his funeral, but God 'introduced himself' to him, told him He would provide for him, and now he was restored to his family and had become Chief Inspector. He told his story with passion and conviction.

"I want to sing a song for you," he said in closing. "A song that has been very meaningful to me during my life". We braced ourselves for something particularly profound, deep and meaningful. He then talked about the wonder of who we are, before launching into a rather shaky version of the song, 'Twinkle, twinkle, little star'.

In this part of the world, darkness sets in rapidly after sunset, and we arranged our makeshift beds and mosquito nets for the night. The stars twinkled, and despite the fact we were a bunch of adults, proud and sophisticated Western ones at that, we found ourselves unable to resist humming a little children's song as we fell asleep.

Next morning, we walked through the village of Opit, stopping off to greet our new friend at the police office. The Police Chief introduced us to his colleagues and, whilst a young man was being roughly searched in one corner, both his hands against the wall, I was asked to pray for the police force and for justice in Uganda. Another first for me.

"How big is Opit?" I asked.

The Chief Inspector sucked in his breath and had a think about it.

"A bit big," he replied, nodding slowly. "Yes, a bit big. A bit big, yes."

He actually told us Opit was a bit big a total of nine times, before his subordinates, eager to help the Chief Inspector out of the tight corner of shame that I had unwittingly pushed him into, offered random numeric answers. We were left to conclude that 'a bit big' probably meant about 340, or 3,400, or more, maybe, or less. But clearly, it's a bit big. Not for the first time, I realised that asking questions that involve numbers is a very Western thing to do.

Back in the dreadful slums of Kampala, another of our treasured national partner organisations, A Rocha, were doing a marvellous job serving and equipping the poorest families in their city. This underfunded but superb team, each member of whom could earn a far higher salary if working in a commercial sector, had committed themselves to providing practical training on some wonderful community and environmental initiatives. They rebuilt public wells and toilets, trained local people on how to build bio-sand water filters, tippy taps (simple and economical hand-washing stations), 'ball, stick and honeycomb' briquettes, fireless cookers (which are like slow cookers in insulated baskets), and space saving sack gardens. They also provided a free-to-access internet café, and trained on advocacy, sustainable farming techniques, and disaster risk mitigation and reduction.

To satisfy their cultural sense of obligation to fulfil a task, one day our UK team was given some practical jobs to do. One was in a settlement called Sseruwagi, where we spent an hour or so mixing cement, laying stones and planting grass in order to protect a new clean water outlet for a natural spring. Word got around, and we gathered a crowd - children and adults alike. A large lady in a shiny silver dress arrived. Mrs Sseruwagi was the widow of the district leader, and we stopped working in order to greet her. When she saw what we were doing she looked totally mystified. "You came to *work*?" she exclaimed in disbelief. "Work again. I want to watch you work!"

The children were also surprised.

"Can *mzungu* really hold the hoe?" they exclaimed. Then their intrigue turned to worry, and the expressions on their little faces became anxious.

"Why are they so concerned?" I asked.

"They are worried that you will break," came the reply.

The impression around here is that *mzungu* don't work, and if by chance they are forced to, they merely buy machines that actually do the work for them. I laughed at how ludicrous this was and condescendingly thought how out of touch urban slum life had made these children. Then, a considerable time later - and with some embarrassment - I recalled the computer, the ready-made meal, and the automatic door. On reflection, maybe these kids truly had got their finger on the pulse.

And yet there was also a very serious lack of understanding within this community that they themselves have skills and assets, and could work towards at least a little relief from their poverty. Some were asking the A Rocha staff, "Have they come to dig our drainage channels?"

They thought that only experts could do any work, and they didn't feel able to do anything because of their lack of education. Lifting the heads of this community so that they gained the confidence to help themselves was the central task of our partners. It was early experiences like that that moulded and formed the values and methodology of the Raising Families programme in my mind.

Leaving the worksite, we carefully weaved and picked our way between a few more tiny dwellings, and found ourselves in another district, another culture, and another language. This cluster of people originally came from a community in Northern Uganda. We were told that they had made their way here having heard that there was some papyrus growing nearby. I must have looked puzzled.

"These people are very artistic," Sara, our host, told us. "They make mats".

Although the construction of Kampala's main bypass had carved an ugly and environmentally disastrous slice through the precious wetland, Sara pointed down the hill to a small area of the remaining wetland, where papyrus still grew. It seemed such a tiny commodity to be worth relocating all the way from the very different culture of Northern Uganda, but political and tribal sensitivities prevented me from asking if there were other factors behind their move.

We were then introduced to the local 'landlord'. She was a large and somewhat lethargic lady, widowed, and with six children. I never learned which properties she rented out, but she also made a little money by running the local pub. For pub, abandon thoughts of your local 'Coach and Horses', and think instead of a filthy, metre high yellow plastic bucket, wedged upright in the mud that slopped between two tiny properties, both green with mould. The bucket had an inch of hazy liquid in the bottom. Male customers would while away the balmy evenings sucking this maize-based alcohol out of the bucket with a metre long straw of cane, fitted with a gauze filter on the end.

"The gauze means they only suck up the liquid, not the sediment," she told us, without looking up. I wasn't sure if she was being nonchalant, or just crippled with shame and defeat.

"Each customer knows his own straw". And I guessed, with that instruction, we were now fully trained bar staff.

The next day we visited the Kiteezi rubbish dump. At the time, this was Kampala's only formal dump site, but it only received about 25% of the city's rubbish. We put on masks, moved among the thousands of caribou stork - ugly metre-high birds with sores all over them - and chatted to some of the workers, who are known by the painfully derogatory job title of 'Scavenger'.

Being a Sunday, it was quite quiet, still with a truck arriving every few minutes, but with only about thirty of the scavengers working the rubbish. Due to the global slump in plastic and cardboard prices, these men, women (and children) cannot earn more than £1 a day. Stories abound of mothers with two-day old babies returning to work here, and of body parts showing up in the rubbish. Dangerous needles and substances are a daily occurrence. Out of date medication is taken back to the city and sold illegally.

My colleague asked one worker why she didn't wear a mask. For a minute she wept silently, before telling us that although she knew it was good to wear gloves, boots, and a mask, she simply couldn't afford them. Carl gave her his work gloves. Instantly, her face brightened up, but she couldn't work out how to put them on until we showed her.

Our next and final field visit was to see the spring well reconstruction in hilly Naguru. This was an ethnically and religiously mixed semi-informal neighbourhood, settled to house military and police veterans in the 1960's, but which had expanded to include their offspring and friends so that now it consisted of 300 families. As a community, it had lost its way. An old spring well had been installed by the French government, but had been rendered useless years ago. A Rocha worked with the local community to create a guarded, self-managed spring well which now served the 300 families, as well as some nearby companies that filled jerry cans from it for all their workers. Muslim Ramadji (short for Ramadan) lived one side of the well, and Christian Jessica the other. These neighbours managed the well, its use, and its cleaning, which happened every Sunday morning. If someone couldn't take their turn to do cleaning duties, they would pay one of a couple of workers 100 UGS (£0.02) as a cleaning fee.

"We have already seen a reduction of cases of diarrhoea and skin diseases," said Ramadji, who to begin with was very hostile to A Rocha's offer of help, but was now a key player in the spring well management. As well as the well construction, A Rocha had also trained 38 families in soap production and provided 27 water filters.

A few years later, I would return to Northern Uganda several times with the Raising Families programme. One of the more remote dioceses that I visited was that of West Lango. We drove past baboons sunbathing by the roadside, and across a bridge over the River Nile. After a couple of hours, we arrived at Aduku, where the newly commissioned diocese of West Lango had its headquarters. There we met the diocesan secretary, Tony, and their young (Raising Families) Programme Officer, Barbara.

The Raising Families programme had started up a year or so earlier when, though an envisioning process, the churches were reminded of their calling to serve their communities. When one church mended the roof of an old man's house, other neighbours offered a mattress for him, and momentum grew. But once more the biggest challenge was voiced as 'high expectations' (i.e., handouts).

In eleven parishes, Barbara had already completed the Raising Families envisioning process with leaders of 187 of their 264 churches. "I also visit them to make sure they are envisioning their churches properly," she told us. "On the motorbike, I can visit four churches a day."

The image of this slim and stylish young women with her striking mane of Afro hair roaring through the bush on a motorbike to visit so many churches was intriguing. There was no way her hair would fit under a crash helmet. I wondered how she was received in such a male-dominated society. Tony read my mind, and the obviously very capable 27-year-old smiled graciously as he talked *about* her.

"She is a great trainer", he said, "but not such a good motorbike rider. Pastors are learning to accept her youth, her hair style, and her dress code. It helps that she comes representing the Diocese."

We spent an hour with them and, as we left, Tony suggested we went home, not via the bridge, but via the boat that crosses the Nile.

"It's a short cut," he said, convincingly. "The ferry doesn't close until seven and, in this vehicle, you'll be there in 90 minutes." It would be tight, but we trusted his local knowledge and judgement and, like the Three Kings, decided to return by this different route.

Driving along single-lane tracks via the town of Apac, two and a quarter speedy, bouncy, bumpy hours later we arrived at the edge of the Nile ... just as the ferry edged out from the bank and into the gloomy dusk. Had we just missed the final crossing? As the reddening sun set, and a million mosquitos came to life, with growing apprehension we asked some locals if that was it for the day. They shrugged their shoulders, but did, rather ominously, warn us that the boatmen slept on the *other* side of the river.

As the ferry chugged slowly across the Nile and into the darkness, we waited to see whether or not it would come back to our side of the river one last time that night. The only alternative would be to retrace our steps in the dark - at least another five hour's quite dangerous journey time. We were eventually relieved and reassured when we faintly made out a great puff of black smoke from across the water. The boat was setting off again from the other side. The ferry was returning. It was properly dark when we watched our Land Cruiser and one other vehicle - a big old truck filled with sacks of charcoal - bump and heave and cajole their way onto the ferry by means of a couple of *almost* adjoining wooden ramps. As I filmed this spectacle, a security guard came and politely but firmly told me to stop. But there's a fine line between initiative and rebellion, and I managed to sneak a few blurry pictures as we crossed over. It took a little more than fifteen minutes to reach the other side, by which time it was fully dark. The ferryboat man asked to use our Land Cruiser lights to guide the ageing vessel to the bank. In a torrential thunderstorm, we drove another thirty minutes back to our guest house in Kiryandongo - a four-hour journey in all from Aduku.

That day our driver, Alfred, drove us well over 400km in the Land Cruiser, and by the time we were back in Kampala the following day, we'd completed about 1200km in the three days, much of it on good roads, but also maybe 200km on dirt tracks, through undergrowth, over rivers etc. Alfred and I chatted easily and got on well, and he told me how life treated him during the days of the LRA in Northern Uganda. Now 46, Alfred had been a driver from the age of 13, and during the LRA era he was held up in a number of ambushes, and several times narrowly avoided death. Both his father and his cousin were shot and killed by the LRA in 1988. "That's when I learned that God had saved my life for a purpose", he told me.

I think it was at the end of that trip that my American colleagues back at the Samaritan's Purse office in Kampala had agreed to arrange our transport back to the airport. An hour or so before we left, we were told of a high alert due to the threat of a terrorist attack by al-Shabaab, the Somalian-based terrorist jihadist group. The US embassy had warned that al-Shabaab militants were planning to carry out an imminent attack, and had told its citizens to take shelter whilst the Ugandan authorities conducted operations against a suspected terrorist cell in the city. All US citizens were advised to stay at home, or to proceed to a safe location. On its website, their embassy stated that they were not aware of specific targets, but that the Ugandan authorities had increased security at key sites, including Entebbe International Airport.

So off we went to Entebbe International Airport. The taxi driver took us around rather than through the city and we were screened about a mile from the airport but, when we arrived at the departures main door the guy checking our boarding cards said he knew nothing about it. "We're always the last to hear these things," he said, and laughed.

Kenya

Most flights to Nairobi, at least those I've been on, have been night flights. I almost always fail to sleep. I'm just too long. It's not only the fact that my knees get crushed when the passenger in front reclines their seat. And I can live with the pins and needles in my feet, caused by my inability to stretch out my legs. But it's when I'm trying to sleep. However high the headrest extends, my head is higher still, and so it spends the night rolling around my neck as though I'm either trying to unscrew it, or I'm trying to headbutt an invisible fly in front of me. "Oh, it must be wonderful to be so tall," I am repeatedly told.

Yes, it has its advantages. But an overnight flight is not one of them. Nor, for that matter the introvert in me pleads, is being invited to speak in a large hall, and being taken last minute to sit in the middle of the front row, with the eyes of hundreds of people either weighing up your potential, or resenting the fact they can no longer see what's going on.

One time, whilst in transit through Nairobi from Rwanda, where I had seriously hurt my back on a building site, Kenya Airways kindly provided me with a wheelchair, and a steward to wheel me between flights. That was my defining 'Does he take sugar?' moment. Ignoring me and talking to my carer, whom I'd known for all of five minutes, various airline operatives asked him who I was, and which flight I was travelling on. Control freaks like me need to be placed firmly in our seat from time to time, and wheeled. It's really good for the cleansing of the soul. I sincerely repent to any wheelchair user I have treated similarly in the past. I have made a point, a commitment, not to do so since.

Particularly memorable on that occasion was an encounter I had with an over-confident and irritable young Canadian, who, having been asked to wait immediately behind my wheelchair for a couple of minutes, loudly and repeatedly (twice, anyway) told the airline staff that they shouldn't be allowing retards on the plane. It was with some satisfaction that, on my excruciatingly painful arrival at my seat on the plane, I found that my impatient travelling companion was sitting immediately in front of me. Retards can still suddenly kick out in front of them, you know, especially just after people settle down to sleep. Accidently you understand.

Nairobi airport has improved over the years. My earlier impression of it was of one long, bland, and extremely overcrowded corridor of exit gates, and where toilet attendants seek tips with as much assertiveness as a mugger seeks wallets. However, in 2013 the airport suffered a massive fire, which completely destroyed the arrivals and departure units. Due to this happening on the fifteenth anniversary of terrorist attacks on US embassies in Kenya and Tanzania, and also due to Kenya's armed conflict with Al-Shabaab in neighbouring Somalia, it was initially thought that the fire was terrorist related. But this was quickly ruled out. Reconstruction was rapid, and the result is a vast improvement on the original.

For all the times I've used Nairobi airport as a hub, only twice have I actually stayed in Kenya. Both times were for conferences. And both times, the conferences were in Nairobi.

For the first of these, I was the host. Others were delivering the content. My role was to make sure that the delegates, who had come from all over Africa and beyond, were well catered for. It was an incredibly busy time, involving the complex transfer of delegates to and from the airport, negotiating with the well-meaning but hopelessly chaotic and disorganised sisters at our convent accommodation, the arranging of off-site meals and tours at places of interest that I wasn't familiar with, and the confusing juggling of many different African currencies.

Various local churches had requested that delegates attend and speak at their Sunday services. Having ensured everyone knew where they were going, how to get there and when to arrive, I set off with my friend and colleague Irina for the church we were due to speak at.

We travelled by taxi to the Toi Market quarter of the notorious Kibera slum, or at least what remained of it, after marauding gangs had razed most of its homes and businesses in post-election violence the previous year. With toothpick rolling around his mouth, our driver told us in slurred and lazy tones that we were in the Forty Jesus district of Kibera. Or did he say 'Faulty Cheeses'? Or 'Fawlty Cleeses' even? Looking it up later, it was simply Fort Jesus. Other conference delegates had been dispatched to churches with glorious, albeit unashamedly triumphant names, such as Maximum Miracle Centre and Winner's Chapel. One was called Overcoming Faith Church, which left me a little confused. I wasn't sure if faith was something I particularly wanted to succeed in defeating.

Irina and I had been invited to attend a church with an equally long but slightly less exotic or confusing name. The Calvary Evangelistic Fellowship Church meeting was in full swing when we arrived, with sixty or so people squeezed into a tiny, corrugated building perched without foundations on a mud floor in the heart of the slum. Pastor Humphrey heartily invited us to introduce ourselves, and to speak from the scriptures. Sensing we were not the star attraction of the day, we kept it brief. A wise move, as it turned out, as it soon became evident that today was Women's Sunday, a monthly occurrence at this church. Sophie, a newly ordained pastor, took the reins, and ambitiously spoke from Revelation 20 and 21.

After their service had ended, we met with the leadership team. All but two of them live in the slum. They told us about their work in the community before guiding us around the neighbourhood. When describing their church and their neighbourhood, they spoke in honest terms about its problems and hardships, but also with affection, pride, and a real sense of ownership and belonging.

Kibera, with over one million people, is Africa's largest urban slum. It started life as a settlement for Sudanese settlers after Kenya's independence in 1963, and these days, we were informed, consists of eight sectors, led by eight chiefs. Many tribes live quite harmoniously together, that is apart from flare-ups such as the aforementioned post-election violence of 2008, when Toi Market was burned to the ground. In many ways, we were told, it has yet to really recover.

All the structures surrounding the church building in Toi Market were burned down during the uprising. "The place looked like a field," lamented Pastor Humphrey.

It's hard to imagine Kibera looking like a field. But despite all their chairs, bibles and electric piano being looted, because of its reputation as a valued local resource and support in the vicinity, local youths defended the church property, and it was saved. "Calvary is not our church", Pastor Humphrey told us. "It is the community's".

This is a multi-tribe church which meets in a 10x5m tin structure, built in 2002. They also have a school for 40 orphans and vulnerable children, the funds for which the bedrock 15 church member families each contribute 300 KES ($4) per month. But this 4,500 KES wasn't even covering the costs of feeding the children, let alone educating them, so the teachers (preacher Sophie among them) and cook decided to offer their services for nothing. Apart from providing the children with education, identity and purpose, this amazing example of sacrifice has strengthened the guardianship of the orphan children, their carers having been motivated by seeing how much the church wants to do for the children.

The church also runs an impressive savings and loans scheme. The 22-year-old youth pastor runs this with perfect accuracy (I quite carefully examined their work sheets) and several small businesses have been established as a result. He took us to see his own enterprise, funded through the scheme. It was a tiny barber's shop (a tiny shop, that is, not a shop for tiny barbers). He employs two young staff members, and charges 100 KES for a haircut.

The church members were thrilled that we'd come, as they'd received Samaritan's Purse children's gift boxes for the previous couple of years. "These gifts are a major reason why we are so well known in the community," I was told.

Duncan was one of the leaders. Along with an entourage of 12 others, he took us to visit his home. Duncan's first wife died with AIDS in 2002, which is when he found out he had HIV. Recently remarried, he and his present wife and nine children (including three orphans who they had adopted) lived together in his home. This we gingerly accessed by picking our way with delicate, careful steps through a fetid alleyway sewer that leaked its way down a steeply sloped track made spongy underfoot by dozens of layers of putrid rubbish.

Though Duncan had lived here 21 years, his home he described as 'borrowed'. It measured about 5x3 meters, with one curtain across the centre of the longest wall. Not only did his family of eleven live here, but it also doubled as Duncan's factory. It was here he manufactured detergent soap, which he sold locally. Somehow, our twelve-strong party squeezed into the house, some sitting on boxes, with the remainder standing bunched together, while the older children shook our hands, and the younger ones peeped out from the shelter of their mother's skirts.

But Duncan had another job, a volunteer job with the church. For despite living with HIV for at least 7 years, Duncan supports other men with HIV from the neighbourhood, helping them to get tested, get purpose and livelihoods. As Duncan spoke with us, modestly sharing how he relates with these guys and the impact this has had, I pushed back a few tears. I couldn't remove from my mind the most bizarre realisation. My deep sense was that despite his surroundings - this most awful, sewer-filled, squalid living environment imaginable - Duncan, with dignity, impetus, and with sparkling eyes, was truly living what The Good Shepherd describes somewhere in John's gospel as Abundant Life.

Rwanda

Rwanda. Small in size, but one of Africa's most densely populated countries. The land of a thousand hills. And, having been there eleven times since 2010, it is the African country I have visited more often than any other. I've taken short term teams there, and donors, and film crews but, more often than not, I have travelled there on my own. Eight of these visits were in the three years between 2014 and 2016.

Raising Families - the programme, or process, I was responsible for - worked through partnership with the Anglican Church. Consequently, among the many good friends I made in this beautiful land were Archbishops and Bishops, as well as influential church leaders from other confessions. Together we made visits to dozens - possibly hundreds - of homes and communities, in almost all corners of the country. I have, most definitely, written out the transcripts of well over one hundred people's stories. Some of these stories from Rwanda feature in my book 'Raising Families – Envisioning the Church to Empower its Neighbourhood'. So as not to overwhelm my readers, in this book I will restrain myself and feature merely a handful of stories from my first, and my most recent, visits.

My role within Samaritan's Purse back in 2010 was to manage the organisation's short-term teams' programme. I would train and equip volunteer teams and their leaders, and personally lead about five teams each year. The team I took to Rwanda in 2010 was the twenty-third team I'd led, but only the third I'd taken to Africa. The team had come together to learn how churches had begun to reach out holistically to their communities. Although by then I was beginning to do a similar work in Eastern Europe and Central Asia, this would be my first proper exposure to this model of development in an African context. Later we would call it Raising Families, a process that I would grow to love and deeply commit to and, in some circles, even become defined by.

The man who was appointed to provide our team with their initial briefing back in 2010 was one Rev Francis Karamera. I wasn't to know it at that time, but Francis would become a very good friend and travelling companion, not only to all corners of Rwanda, but also to Kenya, Malawi, Zambia, Zimbabwe, Burundi, and the UK. I recall some of his words from that very first meeting.

"After 1994 it was said that all the demons of the world had met in Rwanda," he told us. "It was called a nation of 1,000 hills, 1,000 problems, and no solution, but now we have 1,000 hills, 10m people, and hope in God's blessings."

I guess he'd seen enough of presumptuous and ill-equipped teams that had come in their uniform tee-shirts ('Transform Rwanda 2009' or 'Hope has Come 2010')[14] to paint the wall of an orphanage, give out second-hand football shirts, build a house, fill a tooth, and return to the West convincing themselves they'd changed, transformed, or even just given hope, whatever that is, to the world. Francis wanted this team of wide-eyed English men and women to do a whole lot more than take away local people's employment and give away their cast-offs.

"Rwandans welcome support from anyone who wants to help Rwanda become what Rwanda wants to become," he told us. "People will look at you and think two things. You are white – so you are not from Rwanda, and you are here – so you must have cash. But to love is the only thing you can do. The solution is among the people themselves. This is not a handout programme. Give people skills, capacity and support, and encouragement to do it

---

[14] I made them both up, but you know what I mean!

themselves." From the outset I was attracted to this sustainable vision for offering dignified self-determination to his communities.

At that time the Anglican Church was working with almost 900 poor families around Kigali. That week I enjoyed listening to and learning from those who had given themselves to that vision.

Theo was the St Etienne's Cathedral church mobiliser, a role that involved mobilising church members to engage with their local poor (urban) community. He introduced their work to my team.

"It did happen," said Theo about the church's social action programme, "but it wasn't very organised. Then, a couple of years ago, one of the district's homeless girls had a baby which died, and she brought her and laid the baby in front of the church building. The church members suddenly realised they were surrounded by a needy community that needed their support, and the mobilisation programme was born. We started by researching the local area and working out actually how many local street kids there are. Then we tried to reintegrate them with their families, but this was not always easy. Some of their families are so poor and have such tiny properties, that when they lie down to sleep, their feet stick out of the end of the house. But some go back home, taking a skill with them.

We fund small business projects and have also rented a house where some of them can come and live for two months."

We heard about the savings groups that this initiative has started. Clusters of ten or so people, self-selecting, save between 3-5,000 RWF per week, sometimes with the parish match funding or (after at least four months commitment, and subject to a satisfactory business plan) granting a loan to the group. By the time of our visit, the church had granted a total of 5m RWF (£55,000) in loans.

The beneficiaries often set up buying and selling businesses: fruit, charcoal, and crafts. This asset-based approach to neighbourhood development has certainly changed the mindset of many of the small-business women and men that we met, from one of dependency (fuelled, we were told many times, by colonial attitudes and even current-day aid programmes) to a sense of purpose and fulfilment. "We are architects of our own future". The church uses the gospel and scripture (e.g., the Parable of the Talents) to envision the community.

The groups themselves give loans to self-selected members of the group. "We are neighbours," we were told. "We love and trust one another. And this is not just social, its business, so we are not going to risk our savings on something we think won't work."

In this way Christina had started trading. She gets up early and takes a bus to the villages, buys as much as she can afford and can carry, and brings it all back to Kigali. By selling cassava, flour, and aubergines in the city, she makes 5000 RWF profit most weeks. She told us her story.

"My parents were killed in the genocide, when I was 16, and I married two years later. This was much too early, as I wasn't able to complete my studies. Instead, I had two children, but when my husband saw they were girls he left me. I went to church and sang in the choir, but none of the choir members knew where I lived, which was under the veranda of the local hospital. My elder sister had HIV, and I felt I couldn't get much support from her. My eldest daughter lived with my parents in the country. Shame made me drift away. Then a kind priest gave me 28,000 RWF with which I managed to secure a loan for a house, and now I'm back in church, singing in the choir, and I'm a member of a small savings and loans scheme. As well as working, I am studying, and I plan to start an internship in three months' time. I want better things for my daughters. My dream for the future is that they don't have to live like me, but by paying their school fees I'm really hoping they study, take care of themselves, and don't have to beg for money."

Daughters Claudina (14) and Queenie (7) sat patiently by their mother's side on the concrete floor of their 16 square metre room. A banana leaf had been wedged into their rusty metal fence, indicating that non-alcoholic sorghum beer was for sale at this property. "The best thing about the group is not the savings and loans themselves," said Christina. "It is the prayer, the support, the friendship, and the encouragement we are all able to give one another."

As we moved through this informal settlement in the middle of Kigali, again and again we heard the same comment from those who had committed themselves to savings schemes. We visited a food store and a tailor and a charcoal seller, all of whom had very similar stories, before returning to our accommodation for lunch and slipping back into traditional short term team activity mode, by leading a two-hour children's programme in the Cathedral grounds in the afternoon.

I was keen to see how this support process would work out in a rural context, and was given the opportunity the following day, in the small community of Mbyo. I had been invited to meet with local church leaders and activists. While my team did a spontaneous mini children's camp for a swelling crowd of excited boys and girls, I went with one other team member to meet with the local church 'action group'.

The chair of the group, Ishmael, began practically by telling us how their savings groups work. Then Pastor Steven arrived and took up the story. "Our mission is to share the gospel by attending to those who are needy," he said.

It was a heartening tale of transformation, with 25 groups participating, and an average of 22 families in each group. That's a lot of people for one village. And people, I was to learn, who were still recovering from a lot of betrayal, pain, and mistrust.

"You have to understand just how traumatic the genocide was," Steven told us. "There are so many inner wounds, and lives need cleansing before issues of poverty, property, and wealth can be addressed. So, we start with reconciliation, and then when the community has forgiven and begun to trust one another, we move on to social support schemes together. The government now regard Mbyo as a model community for reconciliation, and has given special recognition to the role of the church within this transformation."

He went on. "When the social need of the community members is too great for us, we advocate to the government for their support. But from day to day, our groups save money, give loans and goats."

Most of the group members have received a goat, and they offer the first born back into the scheme the following year. "We cultivate each other's crops, and do home visits to the poor and lonely. The groups are neighbourhood cells. They find solutions for themselves. The savings scheme has led to people owning livestock and doing agricultural and other initiatives."

Until then, the assembled committee members had sat silently, respectfully listening to their leaders, and coming to terms with this mysterious invasion of foreigners to their little community. But, gaining confidence, one of the committee members told us her story.

"There are sixteen families in my group. Every member brings 100 RWF to the weekly meeting (some groups meet twice weekly), where we read scripture and pray, as well as organise ourselves for the community. Each family has now received a goat. We support an old lady who has no children and is crippled. She was so lonely, so we visit her, taking food, and fetching water and charcoal. She is so happy to have friendly neighbours in her old age. We also visit the sick child of an older couple in hospital."

Discerning our genuine interest in what God was doing with them, another committee member joined in. "The wife of a prisoner had four children and no food. Such was her despair that she had decided to commit suicide. But that very day our group decided to visit her. We took her food, and prayed with her. She confessed her plans to them, and the group committed to caring for her until her husband was released from prison."

"Another lady came across the border from Burundi, trading. But she was heavily pregnant, and her water's broke when she was visiting our village. She had no insurance and no money for hospital fees, so the group paid the fees of this stranger passing through our community."

"We support widows and orphans. They now have hope, and the will to live. They are still very poor, but they have hope. All this is getting the gospel closer to the people."

I asked Pastor Steven how he viewed the focus his ministry prior to the commencement of these groups two years ago.

"I led church services, had choirs, we did worship and more worship". He laughed as though he couldn't believe it now, but in the two short years that had passed, his mindset, ministry and understanding of the Kingdom of God had clearly shot through the roof. He looked so fulfilled, so animated, so excited that God had rescued him from a religious diet of 'meetings and buildings', and into a community-based approach to ministry.

"The Kingdom has come to Mbyo," I suggested. He laughed again. In fact, the whole meeting laughed, smiled, and clearly understood exactly what I meant.

After that visit to Rwanda, I continued to develop this 'Church and Community Mobilisation Process' in the very different contexts of Eastern Europe (Belarus and Ukraine) and Central Asia (Kyrgyzstan), but four years later found myself heading up the programme globally, and regularly returning to the 'Land of One Thousand Hills'. By this time, we were called 'Raising Families', and had scaled-up across Rwanda, working through another 515 Anglican churches. Within months, we would start working with yet another tranche of 715 churches, this time unifying Anglican, Presbyterian, and Baptist confessions in the same process.

Many well-meaning donors in the UK still remain intent on merely giving to the poor, rather than seeking to walk with them. Aid is far less complex than development; a handout is much easier to deliver than a hand up. And giving aid somehow satisfies our Western sense of obligation. But I recall the story of a former boss of mine, who lived in a rural African village for several years.

"Bless them," he said graciously, but with a degree of frustration. "The UK donors who sent two containers of second-hand clothes to our village didn't *mean* to put two tailors out of work."

In an attempt to help educate the UK Christian public on what was happening in Rwanda, the big UK Christian Festival 'Spring Harvest' invited us to be their 'main stage mission' in 2016. This involved two of their leaders spending a week with us in Rwanda, and producing a video that is still used to summarise the values and outworking of the programme. It features the story of a lady called Emilienne, who became quite famous around Africa after different churches repeatedly used the video to introduce Raising Families to their communities. I recall meeting the young man who led the action group that she was a member of.

We were invited to view a mud brick house which was nearing completion. As we weaved our way through lemon trees to the half-finished house, a cluster of about twenty people gathered round us.

Somewhere within this group was a young man on whom I found myself focusing my attention. Looking to be in his early twenties, and dressed in a very old brown suit, nothing made him stand out in the crowd. He looked quiet, calm, and sincere. Modest, and attentive. However, it was one of those moments when I sensed the living God whispering to me that He had chosen and anointed him for a special purpose. I would describe this as little more than a fleeting thought that crossed my mind. I don't know why, as he was merely one man in a crowd. So, I smiled to myself when, a few minutes later, this young man was pointed out as the CAG leader. Gideon Rutagamirwa humbly and thoughtfully took one step forward.

"I went on the training," he said. "Afterwards we brought together twenty-one vulnerable families, and together we assessed our community's main challenges as homelessness, a poor diet (mainly due to the infertile nature of our soil), and lack of income. We started meeting fortnightly, to read scripture together, pray and save. We also carefully read through the RaFa (Raising Families) training manual, and tried to follow every step. After saving regularly for two years, the group decided to invest into livestock for each family. So far, we have purchased ten goats, and all twenty families will have a goat by the end of this year. We tried pigs as well, but this did not go so well. We didn't have the skills to breed them successfully."

All the while Gideon spoke simply, carefully, and with an attractive sobriety. Occasionally he would look up and into our eyes, but most of time he remained serious, very respectfully and almost clinically concentrating on the outline he thought we would want to know. "Paying a marriage dowry is a big challenge for poor families in Rwanda," he told us, "And the group has responded to this challenge by paying the dowry for three local marriages, and arranging the ceremonies."

"We also committed to building houses for the homeless in our village, and to ensure that every family is covered by health insurance. We paid for this in the first year from our savings, but now that some of the families have a better income, they pay for their health insurance themselves. Some families live on steep hillsides, which are prone to landslides. The criteria for families receiving houses are that they have children, and also that they have a plot of land. Thirdly, they must commit to participating in the build at every level, not just for their home but also for the others we are building for. Some do that by purchasing roofing materials, and others by their labour. We have one bricklayer, and he is not only using his skills to lay bricks, but is equipping others by training them up as well."

Affirming that this programme was not merely a group of church members doing social action, but was based on their love for God and the scriptures, Gideon's previously solemn eyes began to sparkle, and he concluded with a couple of quotes from the New Testament.

"So far this year we have 12 new believers in our village, and ten others have returned to their faith. This alone is our encouragement to carry on working hard. But God also encouraged us from Revelation 2:9, when he said, 'I know that you are poor, yet you are rich', and from 2 Corinthians 6:10, where we can say with Paul, 'We are poor, yet are making others rich'."

Needing somewhere to shelter in the searing heat, we walked up the hill and into the slightly cooler church building. Here we presented ourselves to the gathered church, and heard more from them about their village. All of Gideon's family with the exception of him and his mother were slaughtered in the 1994 genocide. Shock caused his traumatised mother to be bedridden, and Gideon left school in order to care for her. Others stood in support of their CAG leader.

"Gideon gave me land to build my house on."

"Gideon gave me a cow."

We learned later that this extraordinary young man had also freely given land away to the very people who were responsible for the massacre of his father.

I have met a lot of impressive people across Africa, but if I had the impossible task of highlighting them in some sort of top ten order, then I think young Gideon Rutagamirwa would certainly be in there somewhere.

I made so many journeys to so many very rural communities, covering almost every corner of Rwanda. Hundreds of hours were spent driving, often well off the beaten track, and many more hours were spent walking, when the roads, bridges and tracks became impassable.

On a recent visit, Francis and I had made our way to Gitarama, where we were met by Pastor Alphonse from the regional Presbytery. He drove ahead of us on his motorbike, down into Nyamagabe District, eventually leading us off road and up to Rutongo Parish, where we were to make two home visits.

Stopping by the side of the dirt track, we were warmly greeted by local Pastor Didas. He is a young man who had only moved to this parish recently, in order to be the pastor of its four small village churches, which they call 'schools'. Strict new government regulations regarding the safety of church buildings had resulted in the closure of two of them. Way across the deep valley, I could just make out a cluster of about twenty people, who had found some shade and were resting from their labour in the hot fields. "That's where we are headed," he said.

With no evidence of a road access, there followed lengthy debate in Kinyarwanda as to how we were going to get there. I think my friends were worried as to whether or not their ageing *mzungu* guest would cope with the hike through the hilly terrain and thick vegetation. In due course a decision was made. We would drive further along the hillside ridge, then drop down into the valley, cross a bridge, and make our way up a small track on the other side. A quick phone call to the distant labourers confirmed the arrangement. These days, even out here in hills and valleys that have never seen a telegraph pole, one encounters many people chatting away on their cell phones.

The steep track led down to a small river in the valley basin, where a large, flattish area of tufted grass had two twisted wooden posts perched mysteriously at either end. I wondered if they were they for some form of local ritual or festival, but I didn't ask. A bridge made of logs straddled the river. Francis took one look at the logs, and then another. A couple of the logs had rather a crumbly, perished look about them. It was unlikely that anything heavier than a motorbike had crossed this bridge in years. Alphonse thought that to drive across the bridge would be no problem, but Francis wasn't ready to risk it. Today he was driving the Anglican Province's brand-new Mitsubishi L200 and, as he said, "When you are nearly 60, you don't take as many risks as you used to".

So we walked across the bridge and up the track on the other side. "Here," said Didas, pointing to a gap in the undergrowth. "I know a short cut."

The climb immediately became steeper, and I reflected on how nigh on impossible this would have been for me earlier in the year, when I had experienced a few heart irregularities. Between gasps, I thanked God for my healing, and made the climb comfortably, other than some breathlessness which, at 2,000m above sea level, was hardly surprising. The group of labourers that we had previously spotted in the distance across the valley had made their way to the home of Epiphania.

Entering her tiny one room home, mud built and with zinc roof, my eyes took a few seconds to become accustomed to the dark. It gradually became evident to me that fourteen people were sitting quietly on the mud floor, leaning against two of the walls. These, I guessed, were the members of the local Raising Families Church Action Group.

The third wall was taken up by the door and a bucket, and along the fourth were perched three small wooden benches, hastily brought from elsewhere and set out in honour of the guests. Many of these people had never ventured as far as their capital, Kigali, just two hours away, and to receive a visit from leaders of the Anglican Province was considered a great, almost overwhelming, honour. That a tall, thin *mzungu* was among their guests only added to the intrigue. Little would they comprehend that the tall, thin *mzungu* sat feeling, yet again, and with all his heart, that the privilege was all his.

We were introduced to our host, or rather, the homeowner whose home had become the venue of our meeting. Epiphania was maybe around 60 years old. Despite the heat of the afternoon, she sat propped up in the corner, knees under chin, and wrapped in a shawl.

"I was unwell," she told us, "And the group visited me, and cultivated my crops. I am not abandoned." Filling in the gaps, the pastor told us that Epiphania's husband had left her with four adult children, after which she had suffered some sort of stroke, making her paralysed on one side. The group had paid for her diagnosis, but sadly the doctors were still unable to understand what, exactly, had happened to her. The herbs that had been recommended to her didn't help. In fact, they had made her worse.

"I am relying on prayer now," she said. Rather ominously, the pastor told us they were waiting for 'the inevitable'. Epiphania silently and discreetly wiped a tear from her eye.

The group shared with me how they had built the walls of the house for her, and then had successfully asked the government to donate the roof. They had also persuaded the agency Food for the Hungry to provide a pig for her.

"Our goal is to lift up those who are weak," said Pastor Didas. "We cultivate gardens together, and improve people's shelter. At the heart of what we do is praying together. We also save together, including an amount that we set aside for the poor. We have become responsible for one another." Without being conscious of it, they were demonstrating this strong sense of community right now. Children were caring for one another, and the one baby in the room was being comfortably and naturally shared between its mother and those sitting near her, without fuss, concern, anxiety, or possessiveness.

We left Epiphania and were taken to a second household, a little further down the hill. A crowd had gathered, and twenty-eight of us, many of whom had accompanied us on the first visit, made their way into the courtyard of a home built for another older lady. Little by little, what was now a huge pile of sand had been painstakingly brought up from the valley that same day. It was due to become render for the house walls. We pressed around all the edges of the compound, with the mound of sand ceremoniously taking centre spot. Several women were keen to tell us their story.

"I am Vestine. The group helped me to cultivate my land. I grew potatoes and sold them, and with the proceeds I bought food for my family, and some breeding rabbits. I sold some of their offspring and bought a hen, then a piglet, all from the potatoes! I'm also one of the ladies here who made the bricks for this house."

"My name is Pricilla. I received a hen from the group, and now I have a pig. From the sale of eggs, I have managed to pay for my health insurance and send my three children to school. I also have enough to take care of my husband, who is in prison."

"I am Pauline. I am a widow. I used to live on land that was very exposed to mudslides. It was extremely dangerous, and I was very lonely. When I first met this group, it was their prayer life that impressed me most. Then they gave me a hen, which had chicks, which I sold and bought three rabbits. The group helped me build blocks, and built this house for me."

The CAG leader told us that when they cultivate gardens, they always deliberately leave a hoe behind. Then he reflected on the closure of their meeting place.

"The government closed our church building because they said it was unfit. Among other things, they want us to soundproof it. But the Imams wake us at four o'clock every morning with their loudspeakers, and the authorities take no action against the mosques! But the closures haven't stopped us from serving the Lord, and helping the community to work together to solve their own problems."

As we were leaving, the pastor pointed out a glistening scar on a far-away hilltop.

"That's the tantalite mine they opened recently," he said. Tantalite is used in electronics, and is the cause of much wealth, conflict, and environmental damage, across the border in neighbouring DRC.

It only became evident upon our return into the valley what those twisted posts were, stationed at either end of the flat land. We had parked on the football pitch, and these were the goalposts. A game was going on all around the truck, which was being stroked and protected by fifteen little boys, who were clearly impressed with how shiny and new it looked. In fact, it was hard to tell if they were protecting it or worshipping it.

Morocco

My wife Bela and I had been married for five years, and this was the first holiday we'd taken together outside of our home nations of the UK and Azerbaijan. Having flown into Marrakesh, we drove in our little hired car 60km south, through Tahanaoute and Asni, to Hotel Ksar Shama in the Mizane Valley.

The Mizane valley is surrounded by the Atlas Mountains and, in whichever direction one travels, it involves climbing through mountain passes. The Atlas Mountains have four sub-ranges. To the south is the Anti-Atlas, and to the north the Middle Atlas. But unbeknown to us, we had booked accommodation on the edge of the Parc National de Toubkal, in the Western High Atlas sub-range. At 4,167m, Jebel Toubkal, North Africa's highest mountain, the loftiest peak in the Arab world, and the highest point for 2,000km in any direction, rose just to our east. Jebel Toubkal is usually under a deep covering of snow for eight months of the year (October - May). As Bob Geldof and Midge Ure have surely been told a thousand times since they stereo typified the whole of Africa in 1984, there most definitely *will* be snow in Africa this Christmas time. Even now, in the height of summer, snow covered Toubkal's peaks.

The hotel grounds, known as The Secret Garden of Imarigha, were laid out as a cluster of Berber-styled mud-walled chalets, linked with cobbled stone paths that weaved their way through a lush oasis of olive and fig trees, shrubs, yuccas, and tropical grasses. Set to a backdrop of barren hills, the various shades of green in the garden were only interspersed by randomly placed terracotta pots and lanterns, and by splashes of scarlet and pink from well-tended beds of geranium and bougainvillea. There was a decent sized but deserted swimming pool and a small, decaying and equally deserted restaurant area. The whole site was overlooked by an impressive mosque and minaret.

Unwittingly, we had booked to go on this break during Ramadan and so had to wait patiently until after sunset before being served soup and sausage kebab on the terrace.

The following morning, we drove back to Marrakesh. In the narrow mountain pass we waited for forty minutes in a line of increasingly impatient drivers and their diverse vehicles, while roadworkers sought to begin the process of broadening the road by drilling out a little more rock from the mountainside. As sections of the rock gave way and tumbled down into the valley, they kicked up clouds of thick dust in their wake. At this rate, the widening of this section of road would surely take some years to complete. An old man on a bike, who we had overtaken some kilometres back, caught up with us as we waited in the queue. At this sight of tourists with nowhere to run, he stumbled from his velocipede and approached us purposefully. Within minutes he had successfully persuaded Bela to part with £5 for a small piece of purple agate.

We found somewhere to park in Marrakesh. It wasn't far from the Place Jemma El Fna, the central square in the Medina. The almost monotonous consistency of the coral pink buildings was enhanced and enriched by the colourful produce of the souks - vibrant reds and oranges, purples and blues, all seductively fighting for the attention of the many tourists. We basically spent the day shopping, in the square and in the surrounding souks, for spices, hair oils, black soap, and other random oddities that I had no idea we needed so much. The more the day wore on, the more Bela became skilled at bartering. Having grown up on the interface of so many different cultures and language groups, she had sufficient mastery of Turkic and Arabic phrases to keep the locals amused, intrigued and a little intimidated - no mean achievement in this particular city.

It is true that there were a number of interesting gates, mosques and riads to see. The riads - the traditional Moroccan interior gardens, or courtyards - were particularly impressive. But 95% of Marrakesh's tourist appeal seemed to be built on the souks, where rusty tin roofs and perishing rattan canopies offered just a little, albeit dappled, relief from the burning sun. The traders were very pushy, and some had better grace than others. We were offered everything from henna and hair oil to hashish and heroin. I developed a particular form of manifest ignorance. This involved the spreading of my hands, the shrugging of my shoulders, and the constant repetition of the phrase, "*Je ne parle pas François*", to which the enquiring reply was, "English?"

I would then reply, "*Neit. Russkiy i azerbaydzhanskiy.*"

On and on they pressed for my custom. With forefinger and thumb almost touching, I graphically and flamboyantly claimed to speak just a '*very leetle Ingleesh*', and then confidently spoke what is actually my very faltering Russian with them. This had the desired effect on the trader, guide, poacher, con artist and salesman alike, who would either just drift off in confusion, or wave us away with scorn and disgust. "You Russians don't spend any money."

When we were souked out, we escaped to a café which, due to the requirements of Ramadan on the local population, was exclusively occupied by inappropriately dressed European infidel. A large tarpaulin covered half of the frontage of the nearby Argana Restaurant, where three months earlier seventeen tourists had been killed and twenty-five injured in a bomb attack, allegedly by al-Qaeda. Accurately reflecting the oil that is endemic to Morocco, the restaurant's sign actually spelled out 'Argan' – the final 'a' having yet to be replaced after being blown off by the bomb.

Back at the Ksar Shama, our breakfast next day was a thin diet of bread and jam, identical to the previous day. I asked if I may have an egg tomorrow.

"Yes," was the reply, "if you pay for it". Half board obviously has its limits, and an egg is clearly a journey too far.

Talking of journeys too far, after breakfast we went in search of the small town of Amizmiz. I had read somewhere on the internet and had jotted in my diary that Amizmiz had a Tuesday market. Despite the journey being a mere 32km, it involved crossing part of the ubiquitous mountain range and fording a couple of rivers. It's the P2022, should you know that route, or want to look it up.

First, we drove through a lovely goat-filled forest glade of palms, olives and cedars. Bela picked the fruit of the cactus and instantly regretted it, with its poisonous hairs stinging her hands for much of the day. The road climbed and we looked back over the Mizane valley and our accommodation. The neighbouring mosque and its impressive minaret were gleaming in the sun, but our cottage was hidden from view in the trees.

As we climbed, the mountain rocks became more colourful - red and purple, silver and gold, coffee and cream - and the road became more twisty and ever rougher. It was not the ideal terrain for our tiny, tinny, Hyundai i10. In order to muster enough power to ascend the steeper sections of road we had to switch off the air conditioning and, even then, many times I had to resort to first gear and very carefully pick a route through the boulders and rubble that had slid down the mountainside and were strewn across the road.

Subtly camouflaged against the sandstone, a few almost isolated Berber villages came and went. Their homes were simple, square, flat roofed houses, but their people were few, offering the sum total of three shepherds and one waving child. And not another car could be found.

We were well off the beaten track by now, and a little anxious. We were at the point of turning back when suddenly the road dropped down to a river. We slowly bumped across the part bridge, part riverbed, and were relieved to find a vastly improved road surface on the other side. Cruising the final 15km into Amizmiz on tarmac, we parked and walked through its hilly and dirty streets.

They were packed with what seemed like at least double its population of eleven thousand people, all either buying or selling. This small town, which almost certainly dozes its way through six days a week, heaves with hectic souk on the seventh. Thousands of people from hundreds of tiny mountain-hugging Berber villages descend upon Amizmiz every Tuesday for this veritable shopping orgy. No wonder the villages we had passed through were deserted. Looking the part in her long flowing skirt and a shawl covering her head, Bela bought spices and peaches and water. Other than a glimpse of two French couples, we saw no other foreigners, and heard not one word of English.

However, despite the lack of common language, Bela could identify well with the souk. "It's like a very rural Azerbaijani market", she commented.

After 90 minutes or so we sweltered our way back to the car - the doors, seats and steering wheel were burning hot by now - and returned the way we had come, discreetly drinking loads of fluids as soon as we were out of sight of the Ramadan-compliant locals. The journey home is always different, isn't it. It is no longer unknown. One takes fewer photos, and feels so much more experienced, so much more in command of the situation. Naïve and dangerous as this false sense of security was, we made it home well in time for our next mediocre meal of Moroccan bean soup and chicken tagine, followed by last night's frozen banana mouse.

Another day, we drove to Asni and to Imlil. A little old lady stopped our car in the road and, after moving a couple of tiny stones away, asked us for a toll fee. We gave her 6 Dirham, which was about 50p, and she lavished her thanks and praise upon us, shook our hands, clung to the car for a minute, and waved as we moved on. Having rounded a hairpin bend, we looked down to where we'd met her, and still she was waving.

Imlil is the base camp for climbing Jebel Toubkal. The village is snuggled into a beautiful valley and, unlike the P2022 to Amizmiz, it was a reasonable road for the little red Hyundai. In pride of place in the centre of the village was not a square or a park or a mosque, but an absolutely enormous granite rock which had, as it were, puffed out its chest, folded its arms in defiance, and declared itself to be king of the castle. It rose to the same size as the three storey buildings by its side.

Once known for its walnuts, apples, and cherries, Imlil is now Morocco's centre for mountain tourism. For some reason, today, tourists were notable by their absence. We parked the car alongside the other assembled vehicles - a blue taxi minibus, a camel, and a heavily laden horse - and walked another 2km up the mountain road. The further we went, the more the road became track.

Our walk followed the path of the Rehraya River, which today was serving as a playground for a handful of excited boys, who squealed as they repeatedly jumped off the massive rocks into the deeper water. Women had washed clothes there, leaving them to dry on the rocks and were now walking back into the village carrying an umbrella for shade and with their young children on their backs. Old men, dressed in their white or cream jacquard kaftans, kufi and sandals, chatted idly with one another. As we passed by, their eyes followed us inquisitively. A few acknowledged our presence with a terse nod of the head. An old lady, bent almost double as she laboured under the weight of a huge bundle of firewood, somehow crouched even lower to collect some more from the roadside.

This peaceful and atmospheric valley and village had hidden its pain well. Unbeknown to us at the time, this was the sixteenth anniversary, to the day, of a catastrophic two and a half hours when 700mm of rain fell, resulting in the death of at least 150 people in the sudden flash floods. Forty cars and hundreds of walnut trees were washed away, and large areas of previously cultivated land are still buried under the debris.

What is culture? That is a question I like to ask when training people to travel to another part of the world on a mission trip. My favourite summary of the concept of 'culture' is simply this. 'The way things are done around here'. Whenever I visit a community, I love absorbing the 'nothing special', and am intrigued by the everyday values and practices of people merely going about their daily lives. It doesn't have to be the greatest, the farthest, the oldest, or the most spectacular. Again today, merely walking through a forgotten village in rural Morocco, seeking to respectfully share nothing more than some occasional eye contact and a smile with those we will probably never meet again, this is something I treasure, maybe more than I could describe. For me, this calm and restful visit was probably the highlight of our visit to Morocco. Far, it has to be said, from the experience of two young Scandinavian women hikers who, in this same village a few years later, would be beheaded in a barbaric attack by ISIS extremists.

Burundi

"Got your passport?" The standard question asked at the start of every international journey. Forget your toothbrush, forget your camera even, but don't forget your passport. I'd arrived in Rwanda the night before, but this morning, with my friend Francis, I was due to drive down to Butare, and then on to Burundi for a couple of days exploration and meetings. Francis arrived at my guest house at 9.30.

"Ah," he replied to the standard question. "Good question. No. Now, where could my passport be?"

We searched in his office, we searched in his home, we searched in his office again. With growing despair, Francis concluded that it had been stolen. It was a reasonable assumption. Only the previous Wednesday someone had broken into his car and stolen his computer and other electrical bits, so for this trip he had borrowed the very nice new Mitsubishi Pajero of a businessman friend.

We thought through different options and contingencies. Should we cancel? Should I fly? Could the Rwandan Bishop of Butare (our host on the southern border) find someone else to take me? I was ready to cancel, but Francis encouraged me to continue. "I have never disappointed a visitor until now," he lamented, while I reassured him that he still hadn't.

Over the phone, the Bishop of Butare urged Francis to at least take me down there, and I would stay overnight at his guest house. The bishop had already found a driver (Phineas) who could take me on to Bujumbura the following day. Then Francis found someone in the Immigration Office who was willing to fast-track an emergency passport for him, involving the sending of several emails, the taking of new passport photos, and the filling in of more forms.

Time ticked by. Minutes before the Immigration Office closed its doors for the night, Francis received his permit. This enabled him to travel to the DRC and Burundi for three months. We filled the Pajero with diesel and set off south for Butare, driving through a thunderstorm and arriving well after dark. We were offered accommodation at the Shalom Guest House, and taken for a meal in the city centre by Diocesan Missions Coordinator Phineas, the Burundian pastor who had offered to be our driver down into his homeland. Later still, and back at the guest house, we met with Butare's Bishop Nathan.

He outlined his vision of 'transformation, harmonisation and prosperity' for Butare, which is the former capital of Rwanda *and* Burundi, and the scene of some terrible wars, factions, and genocide over the years.

Early the following morning, we left the mist-soaked hills of a sleepy and now peaceful Butare and, with Phineas driving (let's say) *confidently*, we made it to the Burundi border by 7.15am. I love land border crossings. I even remember when, as a young child, I insisted that my father let me out of the car before we crossed from England to Scotland. I wanted to say that I had run 'all the way' from England to Scotland. On this damp and chilly morning in Central East Africa it was other, more exotic land borders I'd crossed in recent years, that rushed fairly hastily to mind. Thailand to Cambodia. Belarus to Lithuania. Bosnia to Croatia. Kyrgyzstan to Uzbekistan. Georgia to Armenia. Macedonia to Albania.

The Rwanda to Burundi border was positioned, perched almost, on a twisting section of hill road. All around us, the colours were bright. Little homes built of red mud coyly peeped out behind the lavish and exotic green trees and vigorous green undergrowth that clung to the red hillsides. The red river that divided the two countries wound through the red valley below. An abandoned row of black bikes laden with yellow bananas waited patiently while their masters completed yellow, blue, and white customs forms and negotiated the border formalities. Our bronze-coloured Mitsubishi was the only motorised vehicle in sight.

Parking up, we handed over our passports, permit, and vehicle log, before being permitted to exit Rwanda. Two hundred metres of no man's land gave way to the battered Burundi border barrier, where first we were each tested for Ebola - a cursory temperature test taken by an overweight man in a grubby blue and black replica football shirt. Inter Milan, if my memory serves me right. He and a uniformed guard laughed and joked with us. With Revd Francis sporting his 'dog collar' ("We are required to wear the clerical collar when we travel distances") and with a *mzungu* in tow, the conversation soon turned into a jovial, almost hilarious debate as to whether Jesus was a white man or not!

The formalities went smoothly enough, but the whole crossing still took 50 minutes to complete. As we were about to leave, a huge, ugly, box shaped bus turned up, full of sleepy passengers who had travelled all night from Kampala, Uganda. Already almost 24 hours behind our original schedule, we were grateful we didn't have to queue up behind all of them.

As we drove off into Burundi, it was immediately clear that the nation was not doing as well as Rwanda. Homes - some of them nothing more than triangular tent-shaped straw roofs that stooped almost to the ground - were extremely basic. People, on the whole, looked industrious but, if their clothes and demeanour were anything to go by, worked for little reward. The red soil was clearly susceptible to erosion, spilling as it did at regular intervals onto the already maintenance-neglected road. Mile after mile of roadside traders offered one of three products. Bricks (piled in square metre cubes), charcoal (stored in long hessian sacks with extra straw binding to prevent spillages), and bananas. If Rwanda is the 'Land of One Thousand Hills', Burundi must have at least 750 more. These twin sisters, remarkably similar as they are in terms of size and population, looked more or less identical in this respect also.

As beautiful a vista as it was, it was nevertheless tough terrain for the energetic young men cyclists who somehow eke out a living by delivering huge amounts of produce many miles over hill and dale. The nearer to Bujumbura we got, the more of these young men cyclists there were, and the faster and more reckless they became. Maybe it was the homing instinct (and from high up in the hills and from many miles away, the sprawl of the city became clearly evident in the flat valley below, sun-bathing as it does on the north-eastern edge of the hippo infested Lake Tanganyika), but downhill these chaps went at about 40mph, tearing round corners in the middle of roads that were already cluttered with a generous populace of walkers, motor bikes, vans and buses, and which in places had sections that had totally collapsed without warning into the valley below. With one knee tucked under their chin, whilst resting their foot on the handlebar, these young men hurtled downhill on old bikes loaded to the hilt with either three or four wide sack-loads of charcoal stacked on top of one another, or seismic building rods bent at angles around their bike and person. Or huge clumps of bananas. Or great bundles of logs. The most impressive of all were the ones who transported four- or five-metre-high canes, the type used for growing runner beans. These lads didn't go as fast as the others, but how they balanced at all seemed to me miraculous.

If going downhill wasn't scary enough, watching them go uphill was even more frightening. Public transport here is provided by means of the Toyota Coaster. These are the white, twenty-two-seater midi-buses that, with their invincible young drivers and soft suspension, sway and career dangerously around bends, overtaking, hooting, and stopping without warning. Whenever people flagged down a Coaster near the base of a hill, the bike boys would wait behind the parked vehicle. As the bus drove off, the boys would adopt a side-saddle position and, with one hand on the handlebar and the other reaching as far forward as possible and clinging onto the Coaster's open window frame, off they all climbed altogether. Despite pungent black fumes - 'the perfume of East Africa' - obscuring the cyclists' view and destroying their lungs, the bus drivers appeared to do nothing to prevent this happening. It almost seemed as if they encouraged it, daring the cyclists (sometimes two or even three of them) to cling on as the bus roared up hills, swung round corners, and even when it overtook other vehicles, or accelerated down hills.

From the border, we completed the 115km to Bujumbura in a couple of hours. We headed for the impressive Anglican Cathedral complex, and to our pre-arranged meeting with the Archbishop. On being advised that we would find His Grace at his office on a different site, we headed there, but soon became hopelessly lost. Fortuitously, as it happened, as our meandering doubled up as an interesting hour-long tour of the city. Football ground-hopper as I am, I was quite happy to take a brief wander around the national stadium, with its Astroturf pitch, running track and crumbling stone terracing that at best could probably only accommodate about 5,000 spectators.

Finally, we found the Archbishop's offices, in a classy, hilly quarter of town. Burundi's Archbishop Bernard has an interesting if somewhat unnerving surname. Ntahoturi.

"It means 'We are doomed, as good as dead, vulnerable, not safe, and susceptible to disaster'", he warned us cheerily. In the 1980s, he had served as chief of staff to Burundi's President Jean-Baptiste Bagaza. Within a couple of years of our meeting, the Archbishop of Canterbury would install him as the director of the Anglican Centre in Rome, and as his Personal Representative to the Holy See. Sadly, this was a role that was indeed susceptible to disaster. It didn't end well. However, I found Archbishop Bernard to be a very warm and inviting man, and one who captured the essence and nature of our work without any difficulty. Although he encouraged us to begin discussions on doing similar programming in Burundi, organisationally the timing was not good, and the plans never came to fruition.

The Archbishop asked his driver Matthaeus to take us on another, more intentional, tour of the city in the afternoon. What impression does Bujumbura offer to a first-time visitor? Well, snuggled as it is to the edge of the lake, it is relatively flat, with wide colonial style roads, and a smattering of architecturally interesting buildings, some of which have distinct Bauhaus and Art Deco flavours to them. And the solar powered streetlights were impressive. It is nowhere nearly as clean as Kigali, but neither is it a dirty city, with generous attempts at introducing roadside shrubs, hedges and palm trees, especially in the classier areas, of which there appeared to be a handful.

It would be an exaggeration to say that every other person walked with one hundred bananas on their head, but unintentionally my photos make it look that way. There also seemed to be a plethora of unused advertising boards, or at least of massive rusting frames intended for advertising boards. I'm not appealing for more adverts - far from it - but one has to say that the empty skeleton frames also looked a little bizarre. And apparently new to Bujumbura this year are the busy little tuk-tuks, yellow rickshaws, Indian-style, which, despite the faith-filled slogans that covered their rear windows - 'Trust in God', 'Only in Jesus', 'He's the One' - are successfully stealing trade from the city's blue and white Toyota taxis and minibuses.

We were driven up winding hills to see the monument to a hero of Bujumbura at the summit. See it we did, but only in the far distance, as a soldier, with two others as his back up, stepped out from the shade of a palm tree to tell us, "Sorry, but this is a tourist spot, and tourists are not allowed."

We must have looked a little confused.

"Without a permit," he added, by way of explanation. Unable to ascertain from said soldiers where we could acquire a permit, and our charm-filled permit-bypassing tactics failing to change the soldiers' minds, we went elsewhere to view the city. 'Unite, Travail and Progress' urged the sign at the top of a slightly secondary symbolic viewing point. Local children united and travailed but didn't progress in their attempts to relieve me of my cash and 'bon-bons' (which were chocolate and, by this time, dreadfully soggy in the 30 degrees of heat).

Irritated by the children, our driver suggested we leave. So much for the hilltop views of the city. We were driven off again, this time to stop in what turned out to be the car park for the zoo. "It's a kind of a zoo come park sort of thing," was the nearest translation I gleaned from the explanation of where we were. To what end I'm not sure, but a couple of guys walked past with enormous ceremonial drums on their heads. Presumably, they'd eaten all their bananas. At 2,000 BFR for nationals and 5,000 BFR for foreigners, Matthaeus kindly paid the entrance fee, and some more for a guide, who looked grateful to be given a reason to rise from his idle perch at the gateway.

"This is Norman the crocodile. He's 17 years old." Arthur the crocodile was 28 and Jeremy the crocodile was 48. Juliette the crocodile, 37, was so docile that the guide climbed into the grubby pit and sat on her back. I'd made a similar intimate acquaintance with a crocodile in The Gambia a few years previously, and decided a repeat photo was not worth the extra 5,000 BFR requested by the guide.

"5,000 BRF?" I exclaimed. "That's an arm and a leg". But no one laughed, or even understood so, feeling somewhat unappreciated, I also declined the suggestion that, in order to toss them to the crocodiles, I should buy some live guinea pigs and rabbits from a nearby cage. Rather than being grateful, the guinea pigs and the rabbits seemed completely unmoved by my benevolence. Unable to change its spots, a frustrated leopard (or was it a cheetah?) paced up and down in his cage and, in another enclosure, a couple of gorillas swung around, posing for photos and demanding bananas. The antelope had been given a more generous space, with plants and undergrowth in which to get at least a little bit lost. There was a snake house and an aquarium, and that was about it.

The lake was nearby. We drove down and parked by it. Lake Tanganyika is the second oldest freshwater lake in the world, the second largest by volume, and the second deepest. Siberia's Lake Baikal pips it to the post for the gold medal in each of these categories. But this lake takes central place on the podium as the planet's *longest* freshwater lake. If we had ventured down to Burundi's southernmost tip, we would still be only one fifth of the way down Tanganyika's eastern shoreline.

Bujumbura's port, with its rusting cranes and derricks, was just to the north, and pleasant thatched-roofed restaurants tumbled out onto jetties over the water.

"Where did Livingstone meet Stanley?" I asked.

"Just down the road," replied Matthaeus. "Do you want to see it?"

'It' was a big rock, and of course I wanted to see it. Elementary, my dear … no, sorry, that was another famous couple of chaps. After driving for twenty minutes, we gradually realised that just down the road meant about 20km away. But we fought our way through the traffic, under more advert-less gantries, and through the hectic semi-slum suburb, or commune, of Kanyosha. Eventually we turned down an insignificant lane off the main road, where, on a small hill attractively overlooking Lake Tanganyika, was a huge stone into which was carved 'Livingstone/Stanley 25-XI-1871'.

Apparently, it is well documented that they did stay here (the village is called Mugere) for a couple of nights, as the guests of local Chief Mukamba. However, there is a more compelling case for where their *first* ('Dr Livingstone I presume') meeting had taken place, much further down the lake's shore in Tanzania. But one doesn't discuss that possibility around here. It would be bad for trade. This one would do for me, and it was a lovely spot.

An electric rainstorm erupted and ripped its way through the city as, exhausted, we fought our way through the rush hour traffic and back to the hotel. But we weren't there for long. The Provincial Secretary of the Anglican Church had heard we were in town and, having recently become the grateful recipient of eleven containers of children's gift boxes,[15] insisted on taking us out for a meal at the

---

[15] The Operation Christmas Child programme, managed by my employers, Samaritan's Purse.

flamboyant 'Le Flamboyant' Restaurant. The grounds were adorned with exotic plants, huge bamboos and what at first glance in the dark was, I thought, a peacock. It was actually a great crowned (East African) crane, the bird that features on the Ugandan national flag. No customers, just exotic plants, huge bamboos, and a great crowned crane, which Matthaeus tried to shoo away as vermin, and which the waiters tried to shoo back so I could photograph it. It was a wonderful looking bird, which spoiled itself a little by the very strange, throttled sound it made. Chirrup is definitely not the word. It was hardly birdsong either. A honk, maybe. More the clearing of its throat.

Once ordered, our meal took an hour and a half to arrive. I ordered chicken and chips, and my four companions, Francis, Seth, Matthaeus, and Phineas, ordered something more local. When the food eventually arrived, they looked in horror at my meal.

"You could have got that at McDonalds in four minutes," they taunted, adding (when I only nibbled what they all perceived to be the mere edges of the bones), "Who taught you to eat a chicken?"

The exotic crane, having mysteriously become silent and absent for an hour after making all those throttling sounds, led me to reply, "That was no chicken. That was crane".

Back at the Alexestel Hotel, I noticed that another vehicle had scraped and slightly damaged the wheel arch of our lovely, borrowed Mitsubishi. Francis didn't seem too concerned. Matthias agreed to pay the hotel bill, with my money, but at the reduced rate the Anglican Church had negotiated for their visitors, turning a $60 bill per person into a $17 bill per person. What a blessing to receive such kind hospitality - a foreigner who had come with no real agenda or purpose other than to have a look around.

The following day we made the five-and-a-half-hour journey back to Kigali. Breakfast - a huge plate full of fruit and an omelette - came without delay, and we were on the road by 8am. I thoroughly enjoyed the journey, continuing to be amazed by the cyclists and other road users who roamed the main road between the two capital cities. It certainly made the Great North (London to Edinburgh) Road look somewhat dull in comparison. We arrived at the Rwandan border by 10.10 and, queuing with a couple of Congolese Moravian Pastors and an ageing German hippy, had fully negotiated it by 10.40. Three huge roadside adverts welcomed us back into Rwanda. One promoted the environment ('the environment knows no boundaries'), another promoted anti-corruption, and a third promoted beer.

Zambia

Zambia is one of the four African countries I repeatedly visited in my work to establish, direct, and scale up the Raising Families programme, the other three being Rwanda, Uganda, and Swaziland (eSwatini). Zambia was the most recent country to embrace the programme. In fact, my first visit to Zambia was not until 2017. I didn't know it at the time, but I would be returning there a number of times over the next two to three years.

As the plane came into land the skies looked very stormy. We had, quite obviously, just missed a torrential downpour. From the air, my first impression was of the green, lavish, almost jungle like vegetation. With the intense humidity, it reminded me of visits I'd made to places in other parts of the world for post-disaster emergency responses. The energy-sapping humectation of Bluefields, Nicaragua after Hurricane Mitch, and of Tacloban in the Philippines after Typhoon Hiyan, particularly came to mind. Places where you don't *take* off your tee-shirt. You *peel* it off.

But I hadn't come here to respond to any disasters. In fact, none of my many disaster response deployments were in Africa. It was to seek suitable partners for the expansion of the more 'steady state' Raising Families programme that I had come to Zambia. Rather, it was my journey from home to Heathrow, undertaken in a January snowstorm, that had more of a hint of disaster about it. The door of the coach in which I was travelling flew open on the motorway, inviting in a biting northerly wind and a flurry of snow, and dangerously triggering off the automatic locking device on the vehicle's brakes. Consequently, it took five hours and fifteen minutes, travelling in five different vehicles, to complete the journey from my home to the airport. It's for experiences such as this that I justify my obsession for giving myself what others consider to be ridiculous amounts of time to get to airports. For all of the 612 flights I undertook during my fifteen years with Samaritan's Purse, I don't recall missing any of them through arriving late at the airport.

Ndola airport was a quaint, old fashioned, very rural-looking affair. It appeared more suited to the 1950s than to the present day, but the people were very friendly. My colleague Francis and I were the last of the thirty or so passengers to go through customs, and the immigration officer was a very chatty, laid back and friendly sort of chap. As he prepared our on-arrival visas, a couple more guys came into the booth, shook his hand, and looked up. I braced myself for more strict questioning.

"Are you Alan and Francis?" they asked. "Welcome to Ndola. I am Mellbin, and this is my colleague Pastor Omega." Rather than waiting outside arrivals, our hosts had come through the tiny customs hall, into immigration, and walked right into the officer's kiosk! Another first for me.

In his impressive Ford pick-up, Mellbin drove us through rain soaked, potholed, and almost deserted Saturday afternoon streets. Ndola had looked quite classy when I researched it on the internet. I had particularly looked forward to seeing the massive Ley Mwanawasa football stadium that the Chinese had recently built on the western edge of town. But from the air I had spotted large areas of shanty dwellings and now, driving along the main drag into town and despite the wide and attractive tree-lined streets, my early impression was of an old colonial, rather tired looking city that had lost something of its identity and focus.

On my next four visits to Zambia, I always headed for Ndola. And I always stayed at the same charming guest house, with its pleasant rooms and beautiful gardens. I got to know and love the team I would have the privilege of working with and visited many of the churches and communities they served. People often ask me the 'which is the most...' questions. The most beautiful country? The one to which you would most want to return? Your favourite place on earth?

My favourite place on earth is when I put my key into my own front door. I've always worried about travellers who do so as an escape from home and family relationships, and I am, most definitely, not among them. As to the countries I love the most? It's hard to beat those where good friends are made.

The dedicated team of local women and men in Ndola - most but not all of the leaders were men - worked together under the name Kabushi Entrepreneurship and Vocational Training Centre (KEVTC), Kabushi being one of the poorer districts of Ndola. An accredited community-based vocational training institution that offers a number of services, KEVTC most significantly ran a programme of vocational and business skills training to school leavers, and those who had dropped out of school. Through nominations from local churches of various confessions, KEVTC were equipping and graduating 90 young people per year, 18-35-year-olds, in discipleship and development skills, including carpentry, bricklaying and hospitality.

It didn't take long for me to conclude that their skills and their passion would make them ideal partners for the Raising Families programme. Despite the influence they had in their community, and the respect that their leader had throughout the nation, they were humble and eager to learn how Raising Families could help them get out of their training rooms and into the community. It didn't take them long to see how some relatively simple envisioning and equipping of local church leaders could bring about significant improvement in the lives of many families in their neighbourhoods. Although some of the older church pastors still saw their role in quite narrow terms (basically a diet of holding meetings and preaching the gospel, and praying that God would somehow work miracles of provision in people's lives), the younger pastors, whilst maintaining their complete faith in God to bring about change, were also engaged with their neighbourhoods in more practical ways, and were more open and aware of the elements of training and thinking that could bring about tangible community transformation.

The KEVTC team were very attentive, but quite quiet and reserved, and I had to work hard to draw them out of their shells. They even ate their lunch together in complete silence. I began to realise that this was actually an attractive Zambian cultural characteristic, based on respect, rather than a cautiousness with me. It wasn't long before I had the confidence, and the enthusiasm, to suggest we partner together with KEVTC.

Under the 1996 Constitution, landlocked Zambia, Northern Rhodesia as was, is officially a Christian country. Same-sex sexual activity is illegal for both males and females. A survey in 2010 found that only 2% of Zambians considered homosexuality to be morally acceptable. It's 13 million population is diverse, with 73 distinct ethnic groups, each with its own language. Copper mining in the 1920s brought about rapid growth and urbanisation. After its 1.7 million population capital, Lusaka, the Copperbelt cities of Ndola and Kitwe are Zambia's largest, each being home to about half a million people. The nation's economy had historically been based on the copper mining industry, but the city has suffered greatly following the global financial crisis of 2008-09 and the subsequent closure of the massive and nearby Bwana Mkubwa mine the following year.

Bemba is the language most widely spoken around Ndola. 'Thank you' in Bemba is 'Natotela'. However, whenever I attempted to express my gratitude, it sounded more like I was asking for a well-known brand of hazelnut chocolate spread so, in this latest embarrassing example of my linguistic ineptitude, I resorted to English.

The new Raising Families programme in Zambia started just ten weeks later. Until this point, I had only spent two days with these partners, and yet I'd tasked them to undertake a three-year programme with 50 churches in the Ndola region of the Copperbelt. Back in the UK, as I looked through their reporting, it appeared that they had made an excellent start, actually committing to 60 churches. However, I wanted to give them more support, so I returned five months later to see how they were getting to grips with it all and what they needed in order to develop things further.

The long weekend I spent with them was hugely encouraging. They were doing even better than their reports had suggested. They had a highly committed team that had taken RaFa very seriously, the team members often working till late in the evening. In this way they had researched and prepared well, had delivered excellent trainings, and were already seeing the fruit of their labours both in the churches and in the vulnerable families they were working with.

I always tried to ensure a good balance between desk-based conversations with the central team, and quality time visiting the churches and communities they were working with. I particularly enjoyed my visits into the community, visits that included urban and rural churches and their neighbourhoods.

Such was the sense of relationship and camaraderie among the team that, whenever we visited these communities, the whole team would come. I don't ever recall a team member *not* coming to the thirty or so communities I visited. We would travel in convoy, maybe in two 4x4s and on three or four motorbikes, ducking and weaving through deeply potholed dirt roads, sometimes even picking our way through deep undergrowth, seeking to follow narrow footpaths that were most definitely not designed for vehicles.

We would sometimes meet these rural villagers under a tree, but usually gathered at each community's church building. These were almost invariably mud built, with flimsy wooden beams holding up a rusting tin roof, the likes of which were impossibly noisy whenever it rained heavily. A tiny window or two attracted no more than an absolute minimum of light. Inside, these buildings usually had a few simple wooden benches and a table at the front, often adorned with a colourful cloth.

Sometimes the back wall had a banner on it, announcing the ever more elaborate name of the church, the name of their pastor, and maybe their favourite scripture. More often than not, a congregation was already assembled and would invariably greet our arrival with rousing and harmonious song, which would continue until such time as the pastor ceremoniously raised his hand. The congregation, often mostly women, would then sit squeezed together, ten on a bench, and nudge each other and giggle at the long white *mzungu* who was paying them a visit. It was up to me to ensure that I sang along, smiled with eyes of kindness, and was always ready to introduce myself, speak, preach, pray, or do whatever I was asked to do in order to put them fully at their ease. As one who enjoys planning and being prepared, I long ago realised that to pre-prepare a talk was an impossible luxury with this job. Don't get ready. Be ready.

One such meeting was held in a tiny church building with the lowest imaginable roof. It was so dark inside; I could only just make out people's shadowy faces in the crowd. Invited to speak, I carefully fumbled my way up to the small platform, ducking low so as not to bump my head on the rafters. Turning and peering back at what I could make out of the congregation, I realized that at full height I would only fit under the very central apex of the roof, and thus I found myself addressing the assembly with my head almost wedged under the roof, and my eyes peering at them *over* the parallel section of the roof truss. A random passer-by, glancing into the building, would probably conclude that they'd decide to hang me.

Once I attended a chicken presentation ceremony, where needy families were being selected to receive a chicken as an income starter. The church members had committed to giving 25% of their new livestock to poorer neighbouring families. Each chicken was held firmly in the hands of the woman pastor who ceremoniously danced up to the recipient before the chicken was finally passed from one to the other, all to a backdrop of much joyous ululation. This is not a ceremony that happens too often in my church at home, and given their scolding protestations, more bawk than cluck, I think I was more impressed with the occasion than the chickens were.

In another place, the local church had just completed the building of a community piggery, and the visiting white man was tasked with cutting the red ribbon to open it. The piggery was even draped with a purple cloth. In front of a large crowd, a beautifully dressed young girl nervously approached me, holding a colourful cushion on which she carefully balanced a pair of scissors, themselves elaborately bound with some fluffy orange material. In the glare of the spotlight, all the training I had ever completed on how to open piggeries in Zambia with fluffy orange scissors fell instantly from my memory. Whilst maintaining my composure and smile, and inwardly wondering how I could creatively fulfil all the cultural expectations being placed upon me, I held up the scissors, blessed the people for the energy and sacrifice that only they knew they had given, prayed for them and the success of the project, took the scissors in my natural left hand, and sought to cut the ribbon.

Now, as every sinistral knows all too well, attempting to cut with one's left hand, with scissors designed for right-handed people, is not the most straightforward of tasks at the best of times, and these scissors were unquestionably more glam than they were sharp. It took me several attempts to actually cut through the ribbon and declare the piggery open. Cutting by name, but clearly not by nature. I didn't realise that the purple cloth was all part of the ceremony, until a little later I saw that it had been removed to reveal a statement written on a large piece of paper. It read, 'Community for Jesus Faith Mission Pigery Project, Launched by Allan from UK – RAFA 08-11-2018'.

Often in Zambia I would be introduced as 'this great man of God'. I could have been an axe murderer for all they knew, and however much one could put this down to culture, I was never comfortable with this ridiculous elevation of my status, purely based as it was on how far I'd travelled, or the role I was there to fulfil. Once, the young wife of a pastor in Zambia was tasked with introducing me to their church. At the very moment she was welcoming me, and referring to me as 'this great man of God', the rather base thought that was crossing my mind was, "What a stunningly beautiful young woman you are". God help us!

In another place the young pastor became so excited about our visit that he hopped from foot to foot, then jumped up and down like a little boy, and eventually dissolved into uncontrollable laughter in mid-sentence, unable to contain his joy.

"I can't speak any more", he claimed breathlessly, and gave his microphone to someone else.

In some places, the presence of God was particularly real. In one such meeting, the hot sun shone on my back through the open window behind me, and I could not feel even a breath of wind. But at the moment the church leader stood and powerfully prayed for us, a rushing wind could be heard and felt on our backs, and the moment he finished praying, the wind calmed down again to nothing.

One Sunday morning we were scheduled to visit several churches, and briefly speak at each before moving on to the next. Each classroom at the local school was given over to a different church. So, whilst the church I was with was in one room, in the very next classroom another church was in full swing, belting out music with speakers turned up to full volume, and a third was doing something similar just two more rooms away. It seemed quite bizarre to me, and we almost walked into the wrong church. Having said that, there never seemed to be much competition between these groups. There are hundreds of churches in and around Ndola, and I was told that 80% of the population go to one church or another. It's just what society does on a Sunday morning.

I heard so many wonderful reports of how lives and families had changed through the Raising Families process. One by one the CAG leaders would stand and tell their story.

"We found a plot of land and we ploughed it. We then saved together and bought fertiliser and seeds, which are now planted."

"We gathered 20 families and now others are attracted and want to be a part of it. We already had a garden plot but the maize on it was very poor. But all our families donated for fertiliser, and we bought it together."

"We have 27 families and have started saving together. We bought a garden, 50x20m, and have already planted onions."

"We were very happy to receive this training. Many organisations say they want to help you, but no-one helps us to help ourselves. We now support 22 widows. They all used to say, 'What can we possibly do?', and 'There's no hope for us'. They felt hopeless and disempowered, but now they have knowledge they are becoming hopeful and even excited about the future."

"We thank God for RaFa (everyone calls Raising Families RaFa around here). We also now work with 27 families. We meet weekly, and we have plans. We have just acquired some land and we go to view it next week. We're already raising funds to invest into the future harvests."

"Thank God for RaFa. This year we plan to cultivate groundnuts."

Before I left, I asked Mellbin his aims for the next twelve months. He thought for a moment, then replied, "I see a more sustainable programme, an improved community, relational and networking growth among the participating churches. I see a growth of confidence among the pastors, both in their communities and with their teams. I see the church gaining respect in its community, and being recognised as a transforming agent. Up till now, many churches have been noise makers. I think they'll begin to look more like change makers. We're not promising people; we're inspiring people."

I arrived on my most recent visit to Zambia from Mbeya in Tanzania.

Sometimes I travel on my own, sometimes with a colleague or two, and sometimes with a team from the UK. Media teams, teams of donors, teams of volunteers. Despite my best efforts in pre-trip orientation, and my laboured efforts of building realistic expectations, some team members still leave home believing they can change the world in ten days. This is one of the outcomes of coming from a task-consumed culture, I guess. Others, thankfully, travel with more realistic and relational aims. These ones proceed with gratitude, hunger, and humility, ready to serve, but equally ready to listen, to weep, to love. To sit at the feet of those I work with - and learn.

But today, as I made my fourth trip into Zambia in a couple of years, and my first overland, my travelling companions were three Tanzanians. I had known them less than a week, spending a few days with them in their hometown, as you will read in my Tanzanian chapter. They had wanted to discover more about Raising Families from my friends and partners in Ndola, Zambia. It would be good for the Tanzanians and good for my Zambian friends. I felt they could be mutually encouraged by each other's faith and experience, and so had arranged for them to spend a few days together. It would be a very long drive from Mbeya in Tanzania, and the youngest of the Tanzanians, Happiness, had never travelled outside of her homeland before. Despite it being 4.30 in the morning, her eyes were wide with the excitement of expectation, with the anxiety of anticipation, with the uncertainty of the unknown. As my wife told me on one of my earlier visits to her home city, Baku in Azerbaijan, "It's not your clothes, or your looks, or even your need for an interpreter that mostly gives you away as a foreigner. It's the question marks in your eyes!"

We had originally planned to travel by bus. But I was not as young as I used to be, my back not as agile, and my bladder not as strong. And I had a lot of cash on me. What to do? I could neatly call it a risk analysis and then you might think how wise I am. But in reality, I just became increasingly anxious about being the only non-Bemba speaking weak-bladdered *mzungu* on an eighteen-hour border-crossing toilet-less African bus journey. Expressing this concern to Mellbin, my friend and colleague in Ndola, he made me the most amazing offer.

"No problem. I'll come and pick you up from the border."

Now I've happily picked people up from Heathrow and Gatwick airports any number of times which, when one lives in Ipswich - not exactly the end of the earth, although it does share the same post code - can take most of the day. But Mellbin drove an amazing 1,800km round trip to pick us up, one ageing Brit with a bad back, a weak bladder and some cash, and three Tanzanians with good backs, strong bladders, and no cash. His gift to us was the Zambian equivalent of him travelling from Ipswich to Inverness, sleeping for a couple of hours and driving home again, all for the sake of picking up four random travellers, three of whom he'd never met before. What a star!

My three Tanzanian friends had arranged for someone to take us the first 115km, to the Zambian border. It was beginning to get light as we arrived at the border town of Tunduma. There, we overtook a line of 62 Tanzanian-registered vehicles, every one of them petrol tankers that were queueing up at the border crossing. Only one other truck was in the line. As the first tanker crawled alongside us to the check point, it was obvious that it was fully loaded. Fuel is heading west.

Tanzania and Zambia must be good friends, because the border crossing formalities for both countries took place in the same room of the 'One Stop Border Post'. I could not recall seeing such open cooperation before. It would have been impossible to imagine at the particularly tense and segregated Kyrgyz/Tajik border that I had crossed just three weeks earlier.

Thankfully, and despite that massive line of tankers, there were no other cars or pedestrians waiting to cross, so I was first in the queue that morning. First to exit Tanzania, and first to walk across the room to enter Zambia. We had arrived just as the immigration morning shift was taking over from their departing night shift colleagues. The fact that I was their first customer since yesterday became evident when the officer took 15 minutes of fiddling and poking at his broken date stamp before he was satisfied that he had the correct date on it. He took my $50 note, and carefully stapled my visa into my passport. After giving the date stamp a hefty thump on the aged dried out ink pad, and another hefty wallop onto my passport, he returned it to me with a flourish. All formalities were over. By now a queue of six to eight guys behind me were getting restless, as though it were me that was being slow and awkward. I had one quick check of what he'd done to my treasured passport and saw that on this lovely cool ninth of June morning, I had been received into the country on '9 Jul', which was about three weeks after I was due to *leave* the country.

I pointed this out to the immigration officer, who agreed that this could give me problems, and wrote an 'n' over the 'l', and then wrote a little note and signature to explain the error. Everyone being content, I left, and waited at the car whilst my three new friends and colleagues completed their procedures. A few minutes later, just after I'd taken a photo of the building, another immigration officer came out of the building and called me over.

"We have a problem," he said, looking quite serious.

"Will I never learn?" I asked myself. Getting into trouble for my compulsion to take illegal photos at border crossings seems to be a deep-seated weakness in my soul.

"We changed the date stamp on your passport but not on your visa," he said. I was off the hook yet again. I was invited to jump the queue and waited whilst the officer went through the same 'little note and signature' process on the visa receipt. What I didn't notice until a few days later was that he had authorised the amendment with his signature, and this time had dated it '19 Jun'. This time a mere five days after I was due to leave the country.

We drove through the very lax security gates and into Zambia, and into the chaos that calls itself Nakonde. We waited at the vibrant border post for the arrival of Mellbin. It's all movement and transience and shouting and bartering at these places. Borders seem to attract many of those who would find it difficult to work and live anywhere else. I called Mellbin and he said he was on his way. Bless him, he'd been 'on his way' for the last almost 24 hours. But in making the arrangement, I had failed to take into account the one-hour time difference between the countries. He arrived within 30 minutes, and I introduced him to my Tanzanian friends.

"Before we go, I need to get a belt for my trousers," he announced. About eight traders abandoned their hitherto persistent efforts to persuade us to change our currency and rushed in all directions to find

Mellbin a belt. We very slowly drove off up the hill, with tiny stores and alleyways lining the route, negotiating gaping potholes and anticipating one or another belt seller to emerge from some dark corner or another.

When none appeared, we continued to drive off into Zambia.

"I'll get one somewhere else," said Mellbin. But after fifteen minutes of potholing our way south-west, we were overtaken by four crazed men on two motorbikes. All of them waved several belts at us. The belts were flapping wildly in the wind and the men shouted victoriously to Mellbin, as through they'd just caught a fry of prize eels.

Mellbin stopped the car and tried on each of the belts. None of them were big enough. I suggested that maybe he should buy two of them but, yet again, my strange English humour missed the mark. The lads named their highly inflated price, and there then followed another fifteen minutes of heated but unresolved negotiations, after which Mellbin told them that they couldn't just take their friend's belt off him and sell it on for ridiculous money. He climbed back into the truck and was about to drive off when one of the belt sellers pointed out that the vehicle had a semi-flat tyre. He was right and, as we were about to drive for twelve to fifteen hours through the bush, we humbly agreed to go back to the border town with the same guys who would arrange for the tyre to be pumped up. One up to the belt sellers.

It turned out that the tyre needed repairing and plugging, which the vulcanist[16] managed to do with the meagre tools available to him. This gave the four young men another twenty minutes to try to persuade Mellbin that he really should buy at least one of the belts that didn't fit round his waist. Meanwhile another guy was sent running to find a bigger belt and, panting alarmingly, he returned with one the right size. It even appeared to be new. It needed one extra hole in it so, using the same implement as had just been used to repair the hole in the tyre, another hole was made in the belt.

We eventually left Nakonde at 09.35 (Zambian time), five hours after setting off from Mbeya.

We drove for another four hours over dreadfully potholed roads, ducking and weaving our way past Tanzanian tanker after Tanzanian tanker where the roads allowed, before making our first stop to buy watermelon and make use of the bushes. Apart from the tankers, there was virtually nothing else on the

---

[16] Vulcanist as in 'he who mends tyres', as opposed to someone who studies volcanoes, or a particularly logical albeit fictional extra-terrestrial humanoid species.

road; no vehicles, no settlements and, despite us being very close to some national parks, no animals. In the next 900km, we would come across a total of four T-junctions, each of them offering a dusty track that led off to nothing more than a small settlement somewhere in the bush.

We encountered the first of these junctions at 12.30. We stopped for lunch at its grubby little roadside café, called 'Finger Licking Good'. It was by the road to Chinsali. The hard-boiled egg I had been given for my early breakfast had been consumed a full eight hours ago, and my Tanzanian friends had eaten nothing all day. We scanned what Finger Licking Good had on offer, and between the five of us virtually ate them out of business by consuming a selection of meat and potato pasties, two fried chickens and some cold chips. It was one of those occasions when 'saying grace' was more of a desperate plea for protection and survival than it was a religious exercise. I settled for consuming one of the pasties but declined the opportunity of testing out the accuracy of the name of the establishment, rummaging in my rucksack for a wet wipe instead.

It wasn't until mid-afternoon, and with an extra 450km on the clock, that we were first able to celebrate a pothole-free stretch of road with some robust acceleration. This sudden advancement was curtailed somewhat by a plastic bollard hastily kicked into the middle of the road by a policeman who, having leaped from his hiding place in the roadside bush and successfully apprehending us, told Mellbin that unfortunately we were doing 80kph in a 60kph zone. After about fifteen minutes of debate, during which time the bushes once more provided some relief, Mellbin had persuaded the policeman to let us go without paying a fine. We were left quite unconvinced that there ever was a sign saying 60kph, and it sounded to me like the policeman had been forced to agree.

The road conditions began to improve considerably. We passed the Mpika T-junction and Mellbin stopped to buy some beans. I'm not sure if Mellbin really *needed* beans, or whether he just felt duty bound to celebrate the first trading post we'd seen in hours. Even now, most of the vehicles on the road were the Tanzanian tankers, despite this being almost 500km from the border.

T-junctions were coming thick and fast. We passed the third one - the Serenje T-junction - at 17.30 and refuelled the truck from a couple of portable tanks that Mellbin had filled across the Tanzanian border last night. By this time, I was counting down the miles, and the hours. The landscape was virtually identical for the whole journey and, surely, we'd be there soon after dark.

Darkness fell, and we drove on and on. We arrived at Kapiri T-junction at 19.40 (791km). This time we were *on* the T. We turned right and joined the Lusaka to Ndola road. Although it was dark, we could see from the more modern passing cars, and the quality of the roadside café, that we had emerged into civilisation.

"Let's eat something as we go", suggested the ever-alert Mellbin. How he'd driven all that way yesterday, only to briefly sleep and do the return journey today, was both beyond belief and the call of duty.

The café was more like the sort of roadside fast-food outlet you'd expect to see in many other parts of the world. When asked what she would like from the items displayed, Happiness looked a little confused and bewildered, then nervously stabbed her finger towards a cupcake before quickly taking a big step backwards, as though it would bite her finger off for pointing at it. I had made some comment about McDonalds and asked if they had such restaurants in Tanzania. Our guests all looked at me with great puzzlement. This was truly a new experience for them, and especially for Happiness who, despite being a law graduate from a Dar es Salaam

University, had never previously ventured out of Tanzania.

We drove on in the dark, eating crispy samosas and chips (and one cupcake, which never did bite) and eventually, eventually arrived at our guest house in Ndola at 21.20. We were 1,107km from Mbeya, and the journey had taken seventeen hours to complete. I recalled an even longer road journey that my wife and I had undertaken a couple of years earlier, from one end of Kyrgyzstan to the other. That twenty-hour drive had involved negotiating glorious mountain passes, and included stopping to swim in a lake, having a picnic, and even visiting a family we knew for a rest and a meal. But with its debilitating potholes and monotonous, uninterrupted flat and featureless landscapes, the journey from Mbeya to Ndola was probably more exacting. Our driving hero, Mellbin, went home and my Tanzanian friends and I happily staggered to our rooms and crashed out in minutes.

The following morning, the guest house chef offered us the choice of either an 'English' or a 'Continental' breakfast. Evidently, my Tanzanian friends had neither been to England or to the Continent. They all had a nibble at a few of the Corn Flakes that were presented in a plastic tub on the table, before one of them bravely decided to try a whole bowl full.

Another then asked for an egg but, when given a choice, had no idea what fried, scrambled, omelette, or hard boiled meant. They decided for her and brought her a fried egg. Emboldened by completing his bowl of Corn Flakes, Richard then asked for the full English, which arrived as a generous plate full of fried egg, beans, bacon, sausage and tomato.

"But I asked for meat", he said. He nibbled at one of the sausages before giving all three of them to his colleague and eating the rest of his now depleted 'English', with a spoon. Their adventure had begun.

Malawi

It was one of those travelling weeks. Ten flights and five countries in eight days. One of the countries was the green and pleasant land of Malawi. Despite it looking like a mere slither on the map of Central and Southern Africa, landlocked Malawi is considerably larger than Ireland or Scotland and has a population approaching 20 million. My two colleagues and I had two days to meet several church leaders and agency directors in the country and, from those meetings, to make decisions as to whether we could begin a working partnership with them in a nation often described as 'The Warm Heart of Africa'.

The first of those days had started peacefully in Ndola, Zambia, in the early morning cool outside our pleasant accommodation. I've since stayed at this guest house at several different times of the year and its garden is almost always beautifully laden with the vibrant colours and smells of the hydrangeas, hollyhocks, bougainvillea and jacaranda. That morning, its calm air of gentility was rudely punctured by the arrival of the ageing and rattling

Toyota taxi that was to take us to the airport. Its young driver leaned an arm out of its open window, grinning broadly at us, and leaving us to load our own cases into the oily boot of the vehicle. He danced and jiggled in his seat as he drove along to the very loud music blaring from his radio. When I pointed to a sticker in his windscreen which declared, 'This car is powered by the blood of Jesus', his grin widened still, and he chuckled to himself.

Ndola airport, with its ancient half-cylindrical rusting steel Nissen huts, is my kind of airport. In UK airports, like it or not, one has to negotiate the treacherous tunnel of tacky materialism and feel more duty bound than duty free to invest ludicrous amounts of one's hard-earned cash into boosting the profits of Chanel, Hennessey and Toblerone.

Here in Ndola a cat lazily curled itself around our legs as we checked in. No one was manning the one and only security scanner so, after a moment's hesitation, we just walked through it. A piercing alarm immediately notified the neighbourhood that we had watches, laptops, phones and coins in every bag and pocket, but not a soul responded so we shrugged our shoulders and went to wait in the departure lounge, its metal window frames and broken glass looking out onto a barren tarmac runway. An hour later we were up and away, in a

Proflight twin engine Jetstream 41 to Lusaka, 45 mins away. Lusaka airport was a little more upmarket, but not a lot.

A second flight with the same airline, and the same type of plane, took us the 90-minute journey to Lilongwe. We had a six-hour layover in Malawi's capital. There we were met by Canaan, the former General Secretary of the Malawian Council of Churches. One of the great joys and privileges of my work was to enjoy the kind attention of such significant people who, in dozens of countries around the world, would go to great lengths to serve and support me. The following day Canaan was to leave Malawi for a conference in Brazil, but today he generously gave me and my colleagues a great introductory overview of Malawi, offering us his perspectives of the economy, the church and the culture. We ate a tasty meal at Dreamland, a classy outdoor restaurant, coincidentally immediately across the road from the bishop's house, and then through the old town and new city.

Lilongwe is a nice town. On the whole, it presents as clean and simple, but with very lavish government buildings with hotel and conference complex next door. Back at the airport we checked in for our third flight of the day, a code share Malawian cum

Ethiopian domestic 50-minute hop down to the second city, Blantyre.

Here we were met by Victor, who heads up the development arm of the Upper Shire Anglican Diocese. By then it was mid-evening and, not having eaten since midday, we all felt quite hungry. So Victor took us into Blantyre, where we found a small Kentucky Fried Chicken establishment that was still open.

I will not easily shake off the memory of a group of mud-caked boys, almost inevitably homeless, I guess between seven and fifteen years of age, who were hanging around outside the restaurant. In their idleness they would playfully kick or pinch or punch each other. Sometimes in a subconscious expression of camaraderie they would hug each other. And more often than not, their longing gaze would return to stare through the window into the almost empty restaurant. It was a chilly evening and most of the lads were half-naked. Shockingly, one or two had nothing on at all but a grubby tee-shirt. They weren't begging, in fact there was no one around to beg from. They were just there, hanging out on the pavement. Victor tried not to notice them. It was uncomfortable for him, knowing that this was our first impression of Blantyre. To continue claiming we were hungry seemed ridiculous, almost immoral, so we took our food outside and shared it with them. They accepted it respectfully, and we drove off to the tender picture of them carefully sharing out what remained of the food in the KFC bucket.

We headed north-east, towards the old capital city of Zomba. Before long it absolutely lashed down with rain so much so that, even with the car headlights, the road was almost impossible to see. We clawed our way through the floods, managing to avoid the occasional truck that would suddenly loom up in the opposite direction and cover our car with a violent wash of red mud. Two hours later we had made it to Zomba, peering through sodden darkness to catch just a glimpse of some of its colonial buildings, before driving 27km beyond. We had arrived at Malosa, just west of Lake Chilwa and the Mozambiquan border.

I woke up to a quite different setting. Having arrived at the Malosa Anglican Mission Station and Trading Centre at a very soggy and pitch black ten o'clock the previous night, we had been taken straight to our tiny individual brick lodges to sleep. A power cut in the morning was the reason for me taking a cold shower, after which I went for a walk, whilst waiting for my colleagues to wake.

Tucked under the first hills I'd seen on this trip, the Malosa Mission Station was a vast compound. Nestled in amongst lavish vegetation and fields of sweetcorn were various brick buildings, each seemingly having a different function. Around the site were dotted a school, a hospital and a medical training centre, each bearing a symbolic but half-forgotten testimony to the significant investment of pioneering missionaries and their Societies from the dim and distant past. Apparently, David Livingstone requested that missionaries set up a station here in 1861. But looking round this morning, it seemed to me a weary place, an environment where pioneers had moved on decades ago and settlers had taken their place. Dynamism, creativity and sparkle had been replaced by dull order and establishment.

I walked past a church building, and then another, then ten or so chalets, and a dining room. And, unsurprisingly, a tree. But this one was a unique and famous tree, called Chilema, and it took me by complete surprise. Although I didn't know its location, I had read about it firstly on the internet and then on the plane last night, its inflight magazine giving this tree a glossy full-page feature. Of all the trees I could have seen in the whole of Malawi this morning, here was Chilema, in front of me.

Chilema means disabled or deformed and, over time, this one banyan tree had become a whole forest. Its unique growing pattern had caused its roots to come out of the ground and form what appeared to be another tree, the branches of which went down again to form more roots, and so on. Thus, this whole area of 700 square meters had become a vast and interconnected mesh of woven trunks. Before they moved to a proper building elsewhere on the site, students of the Chilema Ecumenical Training Centre had previously met under this tree and their stone altar still remained, looking rather menacing in the centre of this tangled mess.

A hand-painted sign said, 'Welcome to Chilema Ecumenical Training and Conference Centre – A place where things happen.' The strapline didn't inform its readers *what* things happened - just that they did. I looked behind me. I wasn't entirely sure that I was on my own. In the damp chill of the morning, under such a dense and silent covering which revealed only a hint of the stormy skies above, it really was all quite creepy. I'm unsure as to *why* this is a reassuring thing to do, but I sang a little ditty to myself as I purposefully made my way out of the wood.

Back in the open, people began appearing from different corners of the compound, gathering like ants on a set path towards the dining room. Finding my colleagues, we followed, assuming that we also were invited for breakfast. Inside this sparce hall, we helped ourselves to a piece of bread, an egg, some cold chips and a cup of hot water. No one said we shouldn't.

We enjoyed a good couple or three hours with the Upper Shire Diocese Bishop, his PA, and Victor. Upper Shire is the largest of the four Malawian Anglican diocese. 80% of the population are subsistence farmers and fishermen around the diocese' four lakes. Probably half of the one million Malawian Anglicans live in its 32 parishes which have 286 churches, seven archdeaconries and 56 priests. They run 40 primary schools, 12 secondary schools, two hospitals and eight health centres, a vocational training school, a farm and a training school for nurses. Together with other development programmes, this is what Victor oversees on behalf of the diocese.

"The diocese cannot afford a proper wage for me, so they subsidise this by giving me housing and free water supply", he told us later. It really does seem that despite ongoing links with various agencies, including the Anglican Diocese of Birmingham, this massive machine of community goodness is becoming harder and harder to sustain.

We heard stories of people who, despite government warnings and strong anti-settlement legislation, repeatedly returned to live on the floodplains, knowing that each year some of them would die, but wanting to be there so they would receive handouts from the many aid agencies that do flood disaster response each year. I was at pains to explain that our programmes did not include handouts. Our hosts warmed to this approach of local empowerment and ownership.

"If you come as an international agency, people will expect a handout. But if it's just the church telling them to work, the people will just get on with it."

But overall, there was a reserved formality that we never got beyond. Maybe our backgrounds or our visions were just too different, but these good people and ourselves didn't quite click, and if there's one thing I've learned about cross-cultural partnerships, it is that you must have no lurking doubts about your openness and compatibility with one another, or things just won't work. I still occasionally stay in touch with Victor, but these were not to be the new partners we were seeking.

We had a few more hours to pursue one further contact, this time with the leaders of a network of forty independent local churches. Under the dynamic mentorship of a British missionary cum entrepreneur, they had developed an impressive nursery and factory producing specialist foods and sauces in eco-friendly packaging for Malawi's main supermarket chains. Our meeting was undertaken through another torrential downpour, which hammered incessantly onto tin roofs for four hours and caused rivers of water to tumble down the steeply inclined road outside. Once more, we felt that the programme we were able to offer was not quite the right fit for these people at that time, but we were treated like kings and the time we spent with them was probably this trip's highlight.

That night my colleague and I shared a room with a battalion of mosquitos at a local guest house. Waking up every few minutes to smack myself hard on the face isn't my favourite way of spending the night and soon I was sorely regretting the lack of a net. After humans, these pesky little blighters are, apparently, the most dangerous animals in the world, and the wise words of an old African proverb, although often attributed to the Dalai Lama XIV, rushed rather hastily to mind. 'If you think you are too small to make a difference, try sleeping with a mosquito.'

Having spent the whole night with the two most dangerous creatures in the world (humans in general, you understand, not my colleague specifically), in the mirror I counted 31 visible mosquito bites on my forehead in the morning. However, bizarrely, my colleague said that he had slept through the night, undisturbed. Before leaving for the airport, over breakfast he took the opportunity to tease me mercilessly for the fuss I was making.

"I don't know what you are talking about," he chided. "There wasn't a single mosquito in the room."

"I know," I replied, drawing on an old joke I have repeated endless times. "They were all married with families".

Zimbabwe

It had been an intense but enjoyable trip. With two great colleagues, one from the UK and the other from Rwanda, this was the last leg of our visit to five different nations in East and Southern Africa. We had arranged to meet several prospective partners, mainly but not exclusively senior leaders within the Anglican Province of Central Africa, in an attempt to extend the impact of the Raising Families programme that I managed.

On arrival at Harare airport (it was only later that year that it was controversially renamed the Robert Gabriel Mugabe Airport), I had a distinct sense of being more closely watched than in the other countries we'd been to that week. The passenger ahead of me at the Customs point was having his luggage screened, an action that, for reasons unknown to me, resulted in him receiving an extremely strict telling off from the burly immigration officer.

Having completed his rebuke and having sent the chastened traveller on his way, I was already working out in my mind what I might have done wrong and how to apologise for it. But the officer turned to me with impeccable courtesy and a warm professional welcome. In fact, he was so friendly that, having asked me my business in Zimbabwe and the name of the company I worked for, he even asked me if I would give him a job. I suggested he already had a pretty good one, but he clearly wanted away.

Outside the airport, a massive white air traffic control tower totally dominated the complex. I was told that it had been designed to resemble the 11th century conical tower of the Great Zimbabwe ruin. However, in the fading light, I must confess that to me, a mere first-time visitor, I was hard pressed to decide whether it looked more like the world's largest albino dalek or a very pregnant lighthouse.

In preparation for the trip, I had liaised with the Bishop of Harare and with the Archbishop of the Anglican Province of Central Africa. His Grace, the latter, had suggested we stay in the hotel he always used when visiting Harare. He even kindly agreed to book it for us. Having spent the previous couple of nights in very basic and mosquito infested guest houses in rural Malawi, one would think I would be grateful and excited about having one night in much more upmarket urban accommodation. But with our tight budget, and at the end of a complex trip, all I could think of was whether or not I would have enough cash to pay for it.

We were met by one of the young clergymen from Harare Cathedral who drove us to the very classy Bronte Hotel. Despite us driving along what were the highways of the country's capital city centre, the streets of Harare were almost deserted. The occasional streetlamp that did still work was so dim that it only served to create a faint blob of greyish yellow in the darkness above us, its intended impact being lost well before it reached the ground. As we rode slowly through these dingy, rain-soaked streets, my colleague opened up the conversation.

"So, Dennis. Tell us about your beautiful country."

Dennis (I've protected his dignity, and identity, by changing his name) took a deep breathe, before blowing air slowly and deliberately from his lungs. Keeping his eyes on the pot-holed road ahead, he replied with feeling. "There's *nothing* beautiful about my country."

Taken aback somewhat, we waited for more.

"Tell me." He asked. "What do you know about my country?" Without waiting for a reply, he went on, waving his hand in frustrated confirmation.

"Exactly. The president! 80% unemployment, terrible levels of corruption, one decent road, and that's only so *he* can drive down it. There's nothing beautiful around here and absolutely nothing will change until we get rid of *him*."

Somewhat bizarrely, as I stared out of the window of the back seat, that famous quote from C. S. Lewis's *The Lion, the Witch and the Wardrobe* came to my mind. "It is winter in Narnia," said Mr. Tumnus, "and has been for ever so long …. always winter, but never Christmas." I didn't say it out loud, you understand. Purely thought it.

Little did our new friend know at the time, but we were already in the final year of his President's three-decade long domination. Before the year was out, and just a week after the ego-massaging decision to rename the airport in his honour, the elderly President in question would be ousted.

The hotel was indeed classy. It had magnificent gardens expertly laid out with exotic trees, pools and expensive-looking Shona sculptures. Its grounds, although compact, still took up a whole block of the city centre, just along from the Harare Sports Club cricket ground and the Royal Harare Golf Course.

Chris found the hotel gym, while Francis and I ate together. We had a super conversation together and all was well with our safe and gated world. Two more interesting meetings the next day and then we could write up our notes, debrief, and head for the airport and home.

My meal was spaghetti carbonara, and very nice it tasted too. I had studied the menu closely and chosen it carefully. Carefully as in keeping the cost down, you understand, as another famous literary quote, or rather misquote, was lurking in my anxious mind. 'T'was in a restaurant that they met, Romeo and Juliet. He had no cash to pay the debt, so Romeo'd what Juli'et.'

I woke at 3am, feeling grossly unwell. For the next nine hours I was sick, twenty times. On several occasions I fainted, once coming round to find my face pressed into my own vomit on the cold stone floor. Ten times I had diarrhoea. I slept for a few minutes before, or after, each trip to the toilet, then repeat. The tiniest sip of water was too much. Whenever I could put a couple of lucid thoughts together, I struggled to work out how I could possibly put a sock on, yet alone shower, dress, check out and begin the journey across the world to home, sweet home.

Needless to say, I missed the two key visits that were the sole purpose of our visit. Chris and Francis got on with the scheduled meetings which were, according to their reports, among the best meetings of the trip.

By early afternoon I had stopped performing, but getting my mind around simply packing my case and doing the 20-hour journey home still seemed immensely difficult. I gingerly showered, and very slowly walked around the grounds of the Bronte Hotel, just to see if I could stay upright. I decided to give the journey home a go, declining Chris's suggestion that I delay my flight until later in the weekend. When people ask me my favourite destination, I always and sincerely reply, "It's putting the key in my own front door". Never was this truer than today.

It was time to pay up and leave. I was carrying unused and therefore crisp, clean US dollars which, after a decade of ridiculous hyperinflation in Zimbabwe, made me very popular at the checkout desk. And expensive as it was, I did have enough cash, just, and was even given a little change, again in USD. However, whereas my payment was with my gleaming new dollars, the small notes I received in change, also in USD, were damp with filth, stank dreadfully, and much of the writing on them was indecipherable.

At each stage of the journey home, I prayed and thanked the Lord for His help, and felt just a little bit stronger. Our first flight (to Nairobi) left just after midnight. Apart from almost fainting again on the flight all went well and little by little I managed each stage of the journey home, counting them off as I went. Upon arriving at Heathrow, I was very thankful that the coach to Ipswich was about to leave. Two more minutes and it would have gone, which would have meant an extra two hours wait for the next one. I was home by early evening.

On my travels over the years, I had been very sick on a couple of different visits to Uganda and one to Cambodia, had dengue fever in Nicaragua, crippled my back in Rwanda, and caught Q fever from yaks high up on the Kyrgyzstan border with China, but I don't think I was ever more relieved to arrive home than from that trip to Zimbabwe.

Ethiopia

This trip of ten border crossings in ten days started with an almost sleepless night flight to Addis Ababa. For all the flights I've made to different hubs in Africa, this was the first time I'd flown via Ethiopia, so I had pre-booked a simple hotel near the airport for a twenty-four-hour stopover. The father of a colleague of mine, who was born and brought up in Addis, had kindly agreed to introduce me to his city. By extending stopovers in transit to various destinations around the world I had briefly explored a number of cities. Athens, Singapore, Vienna, Warsaw, Lisbon, Vilnius, Brussels and Istanbul all come to mind and, on this trip, I was keen to get just a flavour of 'the political capital of Africa' before venturing further south on my work trip into DRC, Zambia, Swaziland and South Africa.

Upon arrival at Addis, I was relieved to be freed from my emergency exit row middle seat, which had been great for stretching out my legs, but not so clever for being boxed in between a grumpy Frenchman with dreadfully smelly feet, and an ethnic Ethiopian London bus driver who spent all night laughing out loud, very loud, at a string of Ethiopian films. Whilst waiting for my visa I chatted to a recently retired global-travelling football-loving Christian, who writes for Trip Advisor and Brandt Travel Guides. We had quite a lot in common!

Although the visa, customs and baggage collection processes appeared chaotic, I managed to negotiate them all quite smoothly. Then, of course, comes that strangest of moments - the arrivals catwalk - when one emerges bewildered through a sliding door to a sea of staring faces, each one intent on working out if you are their long-lost uncle, their new colleague, the Dalai Lama, or whoever else they'd come to meet. I recall that long ago the young son of a friend of mine, feeling that his father had been travelling overseas for too long and too often, had come to the airport with a sign that simply said 'Dad'.

By now, I should have become used to looking out for random signs that could possibly refer to me. But the practice of airport welcome is a disparate and confusing world, ranging from eager subordinates with glossy corporate signs, to cheeky mates with homemade signs ('Welcome home from prison' or 'Sarah, I have the Imodium you asked for'). From lovers with a heart-shaped helium balloon and a massive bunch of flowers, to bored taxi drivers with a cell phone tucked into their neck, a takeaway coffee in one hand and a scruffy sign mostly hidden under the other arm, as if to say, 'Find my if you can, foreigner. What do I care? I'm on an hourly rate'. Over the years, such signs had been presented to me in various guises. Signs that pronounce the arrival of Allan Cooting, Mr Allen, Samariten's Perse and once, just once, Billy Graham. I've yet to be greeted by an electronic sign. I'm just not in that league.

We Brits are teased for only talking about the weather. But the whole world is united in the etiquette of airport arrival greetings.

"Had a good flight?" we are required to ask. Then "Here, let me take your bag".

At this point we, the complete novice and first-time visitor in a foreign land, completely ignore all the advice about keeping our possessions close to us at all times and meekly give our suitcase, full of all our worldly wealth, into the hands of a total stranger who can't even spell our name. And with that, said stranger walks off into the unknown, at a pace far greater than the weary traveller would ever choose, leaving said weary traveller to wonder if he was the *right* Allan Cooting, or one of several Allan Cooting's who just happened to be on the same plane or, alternatively, he is voluntarily running to keep up with a kidnapper or axe murderer.

None of this happened on my first visit to Addis. The previous paragraphs are a complete aside. For security reasons, the good welcomers and taxi drivers of Addis that morning had to wait out in the car park, but I eventually, reassuringly, found my own name *and* my hotel name on a sign held by one of the final gaggle of drivers. He took me on the seven-minute journey to Lobelia Hotel, situated two small, muddy and scruffy blocks off the main road to the airport.

It was a compact five-story building probably housing about thirty rooms. It had wiggly toilet seats and the screws that were designed to secure door handles and towel rails were coming away. The view from the window was a sea of red and green tin roofs, satellite dishes with their heads pitched up and searching the sky, the shells of half finished (or abandoned) skyscrapers, many with crinkled wooden scaffolding clinging like unpruned creepers to their sides, and the more distant haze of a tired grey and watery sky. But all I ever ask for in accommodation is 'clean, safe, and with internet please'. This room was clean, it was safe enough, and had internet of sorts. Therefore, I was happy.

I showered and fitfully slept for a couple of hours on a very lumpy bed before my colleague's father very kindly arrived to take me for a tour of the city. We didn't stay anywhere for too long, but I managed to see government buildings, museums, a university and two of the cathedrals.

One, the Ethiopian Orthodox Tewahedo Church's Holy Trinity Cathedral, was where both British suffragette Sylvia Pankhurst and Emperor Haile Selassie are buried. Primarily known of course in the UK for her pioneering role in suffragism, Sylvia, daughter of Emmeline, became a supporter and friend of Haile Selassie from the 1930s and moved to Addis in 1956. After her death in 1960, she became 'an honorary Ethiopian' and was granted a full state funeral. She is the only foreigner buried in the grounds of Holy Trinity Cathedral. Haile Selassie, Emperor from 1930-1974 and worshipped as 'God incarnate' by some followers of the Rastafari movement, remains a defining figure in modern Ethiopian history.

We visited the presidential and parliament buildings and the National Museum of Ethiopia. Here lay the 3.2-million-year-old partial skeleton of AL 288-1, *Australopithecus afarensis*, or Lucy as she is known internationally to her friends. Also called Dinknesh in Ethiopia, she was discovered in Hadar, in the Afar Region of Eastern Ethiopia, in 1974. Although she was only a young adult when she died, Lucy's remains were thought, at least at the time of my visit, to be of the oldest recorded human being.

Having gazed at her in wonder, cased as she was in a glass case, later I was a little disappointed to find out that I had only been gazing at a plaster cast replica, whilst the real Lucy was tucked away backstage, somewhere in the vaults.

Next we visited the university complex, including the John F. Kennedy memorial library. Set in a lush and generous site, with some pleasant colonial style buildings, the whole site was given by Emperor Haile Selassie in 1950 for the higher education of the people.

Aside from its breath-taking landscapes, its notoriety as the sacred keeper of the Ark of the Covenant, the birthplace of Rastafarianism, and the resting place of Lucy, it is probably for its coffee that Ethiopia is most famous. Known for their complexity, their pungent aroma, winey quality and distinct acidity, coffee beans, I was told, were discovered by an Ethiopian goat herder in 850AD, in the region of Kaffa. And so, to round off my tour of the city nicely and before returning me to my hotel, my host carefully selected and generously bought me three bags of coffee.

Despite being annexed by Italy in 1935, Ethiopia was never fully colonised. Albeit the capital city of an ancient civilisation, Addis is not an old city, having been developed as the capital from 1886. It is a 'chartered city', meaning that it has the status of both a city and a state. Probably five million people live here; nobody really knows. The whole of Ethiopia has a population of over 100 million. Addis is where the African Union is - and its predecessor the OAU was - based. It also hosts the headquarters of the UN Economic Commission for Africa (ECA) and numerous other continental and international organisations. Consequently, in deference to its historical, diplomatic, and political significance across the continent, the city is often referred to as 'the political capital of Africa'.

Back at the hotel I reflected on my brief tour of the city. From the few pictures and small amount of information I had gleaned before coming, Addis in September was more or less what I expected. The roads were busy, with blue and white taxis competing with green and yellow taxis, as if they were playing out a street version of an East Anglian football derby. The view I had from my bedroom window confirmed this impression of heavy metropolitan hectivity, with much of the city presenting as a collection of half-built skyscrapers, set to a dark, cloudy and sometimes rain-filled sky. It wasn't a particularly clean or tidy city and, although by reputation it is very safe and welcoming, I also felt it had quite a tough, urban and almost oppressive feel to it. Africa's equivalent of Belfast or Belgrade, perhaps?

Everything looked damp and a little mouldy, like it needed a good scrubbing down. I didn't see any buildings that I would call ancient, or beautiful, or magnificent, although I would like to have seen more of the cathedrals. It does have some beautiful trees and lavish plants, but the city hasn't really made anything of them and so they present as a bit random and hidden away in the clamour for constructing ever taller new buildings. It seemed to me that Addis Ababa would probably always be in this half-finished state.

It probably didn't help that, either due to sleeplessness or sickness, I felt nauseous for most of the day. I ordered chicken and potatoes in the hotel in the evening, but quickly regretted it. I could only eat half of the meal and the taste of greasy food stayed with me all evening and half the night. Doing my best to fight off horrendous memories of the food poisoning I had endured but survived in Uganda and Zimbabwe, I was nevertheless seriously worried that I would be sick, but that never quite happened. I tried to sleep but could only do so for minutes at a time. I would dream of food and wake up ready to heave. I felt dreadful and was making plans in my mind how I would manage to contact Ethiopian

Airlines to tell them I couldn't fly in the morning. I was constantly praying and desperately asking for God's healing.

I woke at four, feeling much better and slept again until soon after six. Before checking out I was due to have breakfast, but the nausea returned as I thought about food. I settled for a cup of black tea and nibbled at a piece of dry bread, but then had to abandon it and rush to the nearest toilet. I then checked out and set off in the courtesy bus, really not knowing what to expect from today.

It was raining and I felt very shaky whilst checking in at the airport. I was headed for Zambia, via DRC. The girl at the desk said I couldn't fly to Zambia without a visa. I knew this wasn't accurate but, as she went to check with her supervisor, I was very tempted to call after her and say, "No worries. Just put me on your next plane to the UK instead".

But she returned and announced that I *could* fly to Zambia after all, so off I went. With a desperately overcrowded departure lounge every seat was occupied, so I leant against whatever wall I could and gradually felt a little better, albeit frail. At the last minute, I managed to exchange my ticket for an extra leg room emergency exit seat and felt a lot better as we set off. In fact, I slept quite well on the flight, declining food, and landed in Lubumbashi (D.

R. Congo's second city) feeling fine, peaceful and more or less ready for my next adventure.

South Africa

I was already on a monitoring trip in eSwatini, in the final days of its life under its former name, Swaziland. With my employers being keen to explore new partnerships, I had extended my visit and Wandy, my friend and colleague in eSwatini, had offered to travel down into South Africa with me to meet with leaders from the Anglican and Independent Church networks. Our first meeting was with leaders of the Anglican Diocese of Zululand, in Eshowe, Kwazulu-Natal.

The road south through Swaziland dissected the major sugar plantation towns of Siphofaneni and Big Bend, and carried on through the seriously drought-stricken south-east, to the border with South Africa. Wandy managed to limit himself to one speeding fine in the two hours it took to drive there. He also ducked out of another fine imposed by a plain-clothed policewoman at the border, this time for having a crack on the front windscreen of his Pajero. Wandy is a charming man.

"I'm afraid I haven't got much cash on me today," he offered, most politely.

"Then park up and we'll swipe your credit card,"
came the officer's good natured reply.

"May I pay on the way back please? We are late for
a particularly important meeting."

Throwing her thumb over her shoulder, and with
tired but good-natured resignation, she said, "Go on
then".

I love land borders and, as you know, find it difficult
to hold off the urge to take photos at them, illegal as
it always is. I have occasionally been known to
behave but today I couldn't resist taking a discreet
snap at a notice I spotted, pinned to a noticeboard at
passport control. 'No corpses are allowed to go
through Emahlathini Port of Entry,' it read, before
helpfully adding, 'If there is any questions please
phone Mahamba Health Department at 017 826
6956.' I pointed it out to Wandy.

"It's OK," he reassured me. "This is Golela.
Emahlathini is a different border crossing - the one
we'll go through on our *return* journey. But not
today. That doesn't apply to us."

I checked my pulse. Being reassured that neither of
us had yet to achieve the status of a corpse, I didn't
think it would matter too much if today we *had* gone
via Emathlathini. However, I did spare a thought for
the receptionist at the Mahamba Health Department,

bracing herself every time the phone rang, just in case someone at the other end, said with a very ghostly voice, "Hello. I'm calling from the Emathlathini Port of Entry. I have a question."

Immediately upon entering Africa's southernmost republic, we were greeted by the sight of muntjacs, wild boar and a couple of giraffes, all of whom nonchalantly occupied the verges of the highway into the National Park. We headed east and then south. It was a long but comfortable drive. The scenery and climate changed several times. Sometimes the way was broad - barren scrubland and sweeping plains spreading before us, interrupted only occasionally by examples of Africa's symbolic acacia. At other times the path was narrow - guiding us quietly through the dense and shaded cool of elegant pine forests. It was an interesting and pretty, if not spectacular, journey.

At one point, in a field at the edge of a wood, we saw what Wandy described as 'a very rare sight'. It was a small herd of eland, the largest antelope in Africa. Stopping only once, for petrol and a takeaway coffee, Wandy and I chatted away comfortably, and another four hours passed quickly on the open highway. Pines gave way to palms, and I could make out the coast and the Indian Ocean glistening in the sun, far away down to our left. But we turned right and cut inland, away from the coastal highway, near Empangeni. We were now on the famous Zululand Heritage Route 66.

From here, the remainder of our journey to Eshowe took us past some of the famous battle sites of the Anglo-Zulu war of 1879. A sign for Fort Chelmsford had a particularly familiar ring to it. Maybe because I worked there - Chelmsford in Essex that is - for a number of years. Lord Chelmsford - I had to look him up - turned out to be a Knight Commander of the Order of the Bath. The reference to 'Bath' here has nothing to do with the city near Bristol but to the ceremonial purification that accompanied the appointment of a Knight in medieval times. This particular one of 'our chaps' rather muddied his reputation by foolishly provoking the peace-seeking Zulu King Cetshwayo, an absolutely massive man in height, girth and influence, into war, and then blundering his way to a resounding and unexpected defeat against the Zulu Kingdom. Chelmsford retreated but then six months later somehow restored his reputation back home by attacking the Zulus, mercilessly, in what turned out to be the final battle of the Anglo-Zulu war, in Ulundi, fifty miles to the north.

Time, or the lack of it, forbade us from exploring further. Surely Fort Chelmsford would have been a sight to behold? As it turned out, I read that nothing remains of Fort Chelmsford other than a granite memorial marking the burial site of the 71 British soldiers who died - not in courageous and valiant battle you understand, but of dysentery and malaria. I love my country, but hey, just sometimes …. Not exactly Boys Own stuff.

By mid-afternoon we had arrived in the pretty little colonial town of Eshowe, population 14,744, where the Diocese of Zululand has their cathedral and office headquarters.

Aware of the fact we'd been on the road for most of the day, our hosts had thoughtfully brought us some food from the local Nando's. Slightly distracted by the monkeys which insisted on fighting in the trees just outside the office window, we spent a couple of pleasant if somewhat polite, very slightly cautious hours, talking through our respective programmes, both courteously assessing each other's capacity and compatibility towards potential future partnership. Self-confessed limits to their capacity could be mostly explained by their lack of funds and opportunities, and were therefore not an issue to me. Their willingness to learn was commendable. But I was not entirely convinced that our organisational values and priorities were aligned closely enough to make a wholesome and productive partnership work.

We checked into The Bishop's House. This guest house had a story to tell. The clue is in the name. Built in 1891, just twelve years after Lord Chelmsford's dubious escapades, this was the lavish colonial home of each of the early (white) Bishops of Zululand. Bishops came and went, until in 1968 Alphaeus Zulu became the ninth bishop, and the first black bishop, of Zululand and Swaziland. In fact, the first black Diocesan Bishop in the whole of South Africa.

Educated at the University of South Africa, Bishop Alphaeus was a brave and significant appointment at the time. He had even served as the President of the World Council of Churches, seeking to influence the organisation towards passive resistance, rather than the proposals for violent defiance that were being considered at the time through the WCC's controversial Programme to Combat Racism. Determined as he was in his refusal to condone violence, his role in the WCC still stirred up a storm with the South African government officials who did all they could to lessen his influence by delaying and sometimes confiscating his passport and travel documents. Consequently, Bishop Alphaeus missed several international conferences, making it difficult for him to fulfil his role within the WCC.

His appointment was not without political controversy back home in Eshowe either. So divided was the community that a number of white families refused to allow the bishop to lay his lands on their daughter's heads (as is the custom during the Christian ceremony of confirmation). Understandably, some communicants even left the church and joined other confessions over this issue.

Despite his prestigious role, or maybe because of it, and due to the grotesque and hideous rules of apartheid at the time, the government also refused Bishop Alphaeus permission to occupy his official residence. He was ordered to leave the Bishop's House, and the Anglican Church had no choice but to sell the property. It went through various stages of decline before the present owners bought it in 2005. They have made a wonderful job of its renovation, this seven-bedroom B&B probably being the classiest place I have stayed at in Africa, certainly on this trip. It was an honour to stay there, but an honour tinged with the sadness of its story. Despite the closure of Eshowe's railway in 1987, this property, placed as it is in a town still prone to political and racial tension, was still very much on the white side of the tracks.

We toured the town before darkness fell. Worthy of our attention for longer than we were able to give it, or at least that the remaining hours of light would allow, Eshowe nevertheless had enough time to present itself as a neat and pretty little town. It had started life in 1860, as a *kraal* of our aforementioned and massive regal friend King Cetshwayo, and three other Zulu Kings. In 1869, with the King's blessing, Norwegian missionaries established a Mission Station here, but a decade later, the war forced the missionaries to abandon the station and flee to Natal. For ten weeks, British troops were besieged by Zulu forces who hemmed them in around the Mission Station. They turned the church into a hospital for their wounded and built deep defensive earthworks around the site. After their ultimate victory, nearby Fort Eshowe was then selected by the British as their post-war headquarters and Eshowe became the capital of Zululand. Now called Fort Nongqayi, its whitewashed mudbrick walls these days house museums given over to Zulu history, culture and traditional arts and crafts.

Some say the town's name is from the sound of the wind blowing through its indigenous Dlinza Forest and others that it is derived from the Zulu word for the Xysmalobium shrubs, *showe*, or *shongwe*. All of which was interesting to us because the family name of my friend, colleague and travelling companion, Wandy, who himself is a towering 2m tall and almost as broad and of royal patronage in Swaziland, is

Shongwe. And, talking of royalty, our brief visit was on the sixtieth anniversary of another visit to Eshowe, that of King George VI, Queen Elizabeth and Princesses Elizabeth and Margaret.

We woke the following morning to leaden skies and heavy rain, once more preventing us from seeing some of the battlefields. We had another 400km to drive and so made our way to the highway and the relative safety of the main roads. We were headed for the town of Piet Retief, back up near the eSwatini border, and another meeting with the same purpose, only with completely different people. The town was founded by the Dutch-speaking Boer *Voortrekkers* ('pioneers', or 'pathfinders') in 1883, who had undertaken 'The Great Trek' from the Cape Colony in the south, heading north-east in order to free themselves from British colonial administration. The town is named after their leader, Piet Mauritz Retief.[17]   Retief had negotiated a land treaty with Zulu King Dingane in 1838 but then, with 100 of the Voortrekkers, was bludgeoned to death by the King days later. This led to a bloody retaliation by the Voortrekkers called the Battle of Blood River, where possibly 3,000 Zulu soldiers were killed, and a battle which some say accounts for the strong sense of

---

[17] Pietermaritzburg is also named in his honour.

Afrikaner entitlement and nationalism that had such far-reaching consequences in the Twentieth Century.

In 2010, under a recommendation from the Truth and Reconciliation Commission, the Arts and Culture Minister Lulu Xingwana renamed the city eMkhondo as 'part of the process of redressing marginalisation of indigenous language, culture and heritage'. But somehow, and maybe surprisingly, a number of years later the black community members, at least those I met in the town, tended still to use the original name.

Zanzibar

Uniquely, this chapter does not feature another country but of one of territories I mentioned in my introduction. Zanzibar is an insular autonomous region of Tanzania but justifies a separate chapter on the basis of its status within the rules of the Travelers' Century Club.

I had been invited to Tanzania to visit the programmes of another agency and to offer them some training on Church and Community Mobilisation, based on my experiences with Raising Families. On the way there, I took the opportunity to visit Zanzibar for an overnight stay and arrived via stops in Addis Ababa and Kilimanjaro, landing at Zanzibar in the early afternoon. I bought a visa and collected my luggage (which was almost the last bag to be slung without mercy off the old tractor and trailer that chugged and puffed its way between plane and baggage area) and weaved my way through the chaos to a taxi. The driver charged me a reasonable $15 for the twenty-minute journey to my very charming looking accommodation, the Mizingani Seafront Hotel, where I received a warm welcome and was shown to my room on the fourth floor. With its abundance of wood panelling and a distinctly Arabian feel, and yet within Zanzibar's intensely humid atmosphere, it felt like a case of arid desert meets tropical monsoon.

I walked the tiny lanes of the ancient Stone Town, getting hopelessly lost in the process. I had a map, but that didn't help one bit. I eventually found my way back to the hotel just as the sun was setting, and slept for twenty minutes. I was advised to ensure I put plenty of anti-mosquito spray on but had forgotten to bring any. So, the hotel porter was summoned and instructed to walk me back through the atmospheric lanes to the only pharmacy in Stone Town. This took another thirty minutes, and it was dark by the time we returned.

The restaurant was a balcony at the front of the hotel, immediately across the road from the seafront. Although I had missed the famous sunset, there was still a party atmosphere on the promenade. It was Eid al-Fitr and people were celebrating the end of Ramadan with street festivities and food in and around Forodhani Gardens, just down the road from where I was staying. I ate as much as I could of a spicy pizza (which was about 50% of it), watched boys jumping into the sea (a local party trick, flamboyantly undertaken with tourist tips in mind), and beautifully dressed women and children modestly strolling along. This is a very conservative Muslim island and there are plenty of notices warning tourists not to offend the local culture with inappropriate dress and alcohol. And it seemed to me that the tourists were indeed respecting this request. My friend the porter, as he escorted me through the town, still muttered about the locals several times. "Too much partying," he said. "Much too much partying."

I woke the next morning wondering why I needed so much time here. It had seemed that yesterday was plenty time to see round Stone Town. Maybe I should have taken the ferry across to Dar es Salaam on the mainland or booked an earlier flight. Instead, I booked to keep my room till the time I needed to leave, which was about 7pm.

After a decent buffet breakfast (during which time I rather bizarrely stumbled across a nicely written internet article about the demise of Lowestoft), I walked the 100m up the road to the port. Across the road from the port entrance was the Old Dispensary, a wonderful colonial building built in the late 19th century by Ismaili Indian merchant Tharia Topan as a hospital in celebration of Queen Victoria. After wandering around its corridors (off which some rooms are being used as offices for NGOs) I got chatting to a guy who eventually persuaded me to go on the Spice Tour.

"For $30 I will take you and show you round the spice farm."

"Maybe for $20", I suggested.

"No, $25 for the taxi and $5 for the entrance fee."

I agreed and he did a deal with a nearby taxi driver. After a few hundred yards of driving he said, "I'll get out here and leave you with the driver. He speaks good English."

And with that he was gone. The driver did speak good English, and all was well, although later, when I gave him $25 ('your friend said $25 for the taxi and another $5 for the entrance fee') he was visibly upset. Not knowing the details of the deal he had made in Swahili with the tout, I decided to relent and gave him $30 anyway.

Similar things happened at the Spice Farm and I ended up giving $30 to the guide, tips to two other young men (one for cutting open some fruits for me and the other for splicing trees so I could sample the spices) and bought a couple of oils and one packet of spice.

However, despite blowing my meagre budget, I really enjoyed my time there. I was shown around by

Mohammed, one of the leading men in the co-operative. Halfway through the tour, a younger guide came up to him and briefly spoke with him in Swahili.

"Do you know what he was saying?" he asked me, as the young man walked away. "We had a phone call to tell us you were coming, and that we must treat you with great respect. That's why I am showing you round personally."

Highly unlikely, I think, unless my friend the tout had developed a conscience after abandoning me in the taxi. But Mohammed was a good guide and, when he learned what work I did, he wanted me to meet the co-operative leaders. He did seem genuinely interested in anything that I could bring to the co-op to help them become more sustainable, but equally, representing an international NGO has often won me new friends who have grant-potential in their eyes.

I saw cinnamon, both sliced from the tree (for making cinnamon sticks) and from crushed leaves. Even the roots are used like menthol for their breathing properties. "But if you visit my house and smell cinnamon coming from the windows, whatever you do don't knock on the door".

"Because there is sickness in the house?" I asked, naively as it turned out.

"No, because mother and father will be in the house, making babies."

The turmeric rhizomes are used for colouring hot curries (which typically around here also include a mix of ginger, chili, cloves and pepper) and to counteract skin infections.

Next, I had a lesson on parasitic and symbiotic plants; those that cling to others, either for good or for harm. Vanilla is symbiotic; when green it has no smell, but when yellow it has a strong smell and is ready for harvesting. Most crops are harvested twice a year but vanilla just once.

The boy crushed some lemon grass for me to smell. It is used in green tea ('*mchai*' in Swahili) and is praised for repelling mosquitos, especially when burned in the evenings. When mixed with coconut oil it is used for improving complexion.

I learned that horse plant gives clearer vision for those with cataracts, and tapioca leaves improve blood circulation. Cardamom is called the 'Queen of Spice' and is used as the base for all masala dishes. When eaten with beans it reduces flatulence, apparently (which is helpful to know!), and men who have been out drinking take it to lessen the smell of alcohol on their breath before they go home.

At this point I was urgently compelled to wonder what they had for caterpillar bites. One of these pesky creatures had dropped from a tree and gave me a belting sting on my neck, then fell down inside my shirt and gave me a second belting bite on my shoulder. I had to take my shirt off and brush it away to the floor. A tiny little thing, but vicious.

I was shown ginger (used for anti-sickness and male potency), cloves and ylang-ylang (from the cananga tree and used in Chanel No 5) and bought vanilla and ylang-ylang samples at $5 each, before trying various fruits (mandarin, banana, red banana, pineapple, and various others I can't recall).

Mohammed walked me back to the taxi and was clearly interested in staying in touch. But I stopped short of exchanging cards and phone numbers, explaining that it was unlikely that I would be in these parts again.

My taxi driver had been patiently waiting for almost two hours. We chatted on the way back to town. We drove behind several dala-dalas, the small flatbed trucks with a cage on the back which holds twenty or so paying passengers. Young men stood clinging on the back of some of those that had no more room in the cage.

"If the police catch them, it's only a small fine; about $5 dollars," he said.

"Dollar dollar, dala dala", I suggested. He laughed. No, really. He laughed.

"What's the name of this town?" I asked him as we hit the junction for the main road back to Zanzibar City.

"Bububu", he replied, then laughed again.

"What does that mean in Swahili?" I asked.

He laughed yet again. "Nothing!" he replied. "Zanzibar's earliest railway used to run through here (in 1905), and bu-bu-bu was the sound the trains made."

I told him about the town of Smell No Taste in Liberia, which made him totally crack up and almost collide with a dala-dala.

Entering into Zanzibar City we had to circle round Stone Town due to its one-way system. That gave me the opportunity to see some more of the town and particularly an interesting neighbourhood called Michenzani in Ng'ambo ('The Other Side') which included vast blocks of 5-7 floor government housing which, I was told, were 'built a long while ago for the poor'. It all looked very Soviet, although I had thought that the Soviet Union had little real influence in Tanzania's post-independence socialist days. Later, when researching these apartment blocks a little more, I read that they were built in the late 1960s and early 1970s, with the aid of the (East) German Democratic Republic. They are called *Plattenbauten*, and apparently these days, due to low water pressure, only the lowest two floors receive running water.

Back at the hotel I lunched on a toasted cheese and tomato sandwich which sadly came dripping with mayonnaise. Nothing ruins and good cheese and tomato sandwich more. Four girls, I guessed about twenty years old, sat on the next table. Each of them was dressed in full black attire, although one pushed back her hijab when sitting at the table. My best guess was that they were from Dar es Salaam. They were nationals, Muslims, ethnically probably two Tanzanians and two Indians but, somehow, they didn't strike me as locals. They were getting to know one another and spoke mostly in English. At one point, they were talking about their dress code.

"Sometimes I wear jeans," said one.

Another of the girls replied with a serious question. "Really? What does your father have to say about that? Does he allow you to?"

"Yes, he's OK about it really." The first girl looked visibly shocked and spent the next ten minutes staring thoughtfully into the mid-distance. This confession of modernism had obviously seriously rocked her.

At 3pm I went walking round Stone Town again, once more getting well and truly lost in its tiny lanes and atmospheric alleys. I felt completely safe and relaxed, despite groups of idle, staring men and lads clustering around doorways and pavements. I wasn't so relaxed when a couple of 'tour guides' wouldn't accept no for an answer. They started off with some really friendly chat and although most backed off when it became clear I didn't want a guide, James just would not take no for an answer. His starting price was $25, just to take me to the old Slave Market at the nearby Anglican Church. It's true that I had been aiming for it anyway and however lost I was, I still felt confident that I would find it in the end. But he tried every emotional tactic, from my need for his local expertise and historic knowledge, right through to shameless and aggressive begging, telling me how he hadn't eaten all day. He was quite disgruntled when I eventually, quite firmly, had to tell him to go away.

I did find the Anglican Cathedral and Slave Market and paid the $5 entrance fee to look round. Zanzibar was one of the last places in the world where slavery was abolished and the conditions those poor incarcerated people had to stay in whilst waiting to be sold in the market were *awful*.

I made my way back to the hotel by 5pm and watched the sun set whilst eating tomato soup and chips and drinking a cappuccino on the balcony. The taxi driver that I had booked for $10 to take me to the airport, I somehow doubted would come, but there he was, just outside the foyer of the hotel and we were on our way to the airport by 7pm. We had a good chat about Eid al-Fitr, gifts for the poor, Zanzibar's independence, and Brexit, and he didn't seek any more money from me - a welcome relief from several other of my more pressured experiences earlier in the day. The tourist in me was replete. I was on my way to Tanzania proper.

Tanzania

In an age when we marvel at the possibility of sitting
on a plane for 19 hours and travelling nonstop for
9,500 miles, I must confess that I'm equally
intrigued by the world's *shortest* commercial flight.
This, I am told, is scheduled to last for just 90
seconds. Given a decent tail wind, one could even
expect to complete the 1.7-mile hop between the two
Orkney Islands of Westray (population: 640) and
Papa Westray (population: 72) in less than a minute.

The shortest commercial flight I can recall having
been on took a little longer. Just over a quarter of
an hour. As it typically takes me about 90 minutes
to work out how to use the in-flight entertainment
and another hour gingerly to take the foil wrapper off
the chicken and pasta meal in a way that doesn't
cast it spinning horizontally across the fuselage and
into the lap of an unsuspecting businessman, it was
probably a blessing that neither film nor food was
available.

I was leaving the autonomous region of Zanzibar and
making my way to Tanzania proper. Zanzibar's
airport was simple, clean and efficient, although the

departure lounge was so hot and damp that within minutes my clothes were sticking to me. My flight took off early, was not long enough to be eventful, and landed at about the time it was due to take off. Consequently, I had collected my luggage, taken a taxi and arrived at my prebooked Best Western Hotel in the Central Business District of Dar es Salaam a good 90 minutes earlier than I had anticipated.

"Mr Cutting!" The girl on the reception desk welcomed me, as though she already knew me well but hadn't anticipated seeing me at her hotel. I felt like a rock star on an unscheduled visit.

"We had a taxi waiting for you at the airport!" Before leaving home, I had enquired about airport transfers but not actually booked one.

"Don't worry," she said cheerily, as I profusely apologised for the confusion. "We thought we'd send one for you just in case."

I can't help it. Whenever I stay in a multi-storey building, I feel compelled to press the button on the lift which will take me to the highest point, be it accessible to the public or not. The best view in the house. In the Best Western, my room was on the fourth floor but there were plenty more floors above me. Therefore, true to form and soon after dawn the following morning, I climbed the hotel stairs and managed to squeeze through a glass door that was wedged ajar and stepped into a derelict, dusty and deserted gym. There, spread before me, was my personal, sneak, 360-degree view of the city.

Unsurprisingly, Dar es Salaam is by far the largest city in Tanzania, although not its capital. What I hadn't realised is that it is the fifth most populous administrative area in the whole of Africa.[18] As such, one would expect it to struggle to live up to its name which translates as 'the house, or haven, of peace'. But at dawn, from this penthouse vista, all seemed quite calm. Having fought and choked my way, many times and for hour after hour, through the horrific traffic jams of Nairobi and Kampala, this was not what I expected. Not exactly a haven of peace, but surprisingly calm for a Monday morning.

I looked down onto the railway line immediately outside the hotel's boundary fence. A functioning commuter train weaved its way through what was basically a railway scrapyard, like a snake sliding through rotting vegetation. Half dismantled, half derailed carriages and redundant marshalling sheds stood, or tottered, as a silent reminder of better times. A family of vervet monkeys occupied one of the rusting shed roofs, father protectively keeping

---

[18] In case you are wondering, Lagos is the biggest, followed by Cairo, Kinshasa-Brazzaville, and Johannesburg.

watch over the area and mother attending more specifically to her playful and fearless young.

Alongside the railway line, I spotted evidence of early construction works on the proposed standard gauge railway line that will fly-over the city and on, ultimately and ambitiously, into the neighbouring countries of Rwanda, Uganda, Burundi, and the DRC. To my left I could see some ships in the harbour and others in the port. Huge new blue and gold skyscrapers in the Central Business District dominated the skyline. They looked down proudly on their neighbouring, more modest, pink, cream and grey high-rise apartments, their flat roofs covered with satellite dishes, water tanks and heavily laden clothes lines. To my right, the 60,000-seater Benjamin Mkapa national sports stadium had settled like a massive spaceship or an oval cookie cutter into the surrounding landscape.

It was time to go to work. Up till then it had all been travelling and tourism. Even this morning would be all travelling. I took a taxi to Dar es Salaam airport, 40 minutes away. My domestic flight to Mbeya took just under 90 minutes. The reason for my visit was to get to know the Grassroots Trust team and their mission which, using their smallish network of churches, is to support hundreds of children and families by means of education and a feeding programme. Once I'd seen their work, three of their leaders were the ones I'd planned to take over to Zambia to introduce to my friends and colleagues in Ndola, where they would receive training in the community development methodology that we use within our Raising Families programme.

At the recently built Mbeya airport about fifty tiny children, resplendently smothered in their over-sized green and red school uniforms, were waiting excitedly to greet the passengers. 'How cute', was my first thought. But then I had a second thought. I knew my new friends in Mbeya had a thriving child sponsorship programme. Had they arranged this reception just for me? 'Be ready for anything,' I told myself. It wouldn't be the first time I'd received such a lavish and personalised welcome, and I knew all too well that such greetings required a response, be it to preach a sermon, sing a song or, heaven forbid, perform a dance. I simply waved at the cuties, just in case it was me they had come to see. But this time, I was told when collecting my bags, the children were purely here as a school outing, to see the plane land. More relieved than embarrassed or disappointed, I comfortably sank back into my anonymity. My real hosts were waiting, more modestly, in the arrival area. Being the only *mzungu* in the airport, it took very little effort on their part to work out 'was it me they were looking for'. Hello.

The drive into the city took about half an hour, thirty minutes during which I struggled to understand anything that their main man, Richard, was saying to me. He and his colleagues chatted and joked comfortably between themselves but seemed as though they didn't quite know what to do with me. I sat back and relaxed. Experience had taught me to ride the first hour or two, emotionally, relationally, and everything would work out fine.

The road was in good condition, almost straight, with open fields that gave way to the charming backdrop of the Mbeya Hills. I wonder what altitude we are at. I dared to ask. After a long discussion, it was concluded that no one knew. Or, if they did, I didn't understand their answer. Or they didn't understand my question. I smiled a mild rebuke to myself. Yet another very Western question, Alan. How much, how many, how high, how long, how old? Silly boy. Looking it up later, I discovered that Mbeya is located at a quite impressive 1,700m.

The vehicle of choice here is the tuk-tuk, or *bijaj*, in local parlance. These little auto-rickshaws come in every bright colour imaginable. There are thousands of the things buzzing around Mbeya like colourful, albeit expensive bees. Apparently, when new, they cost up to $4,000, but not many were new.

I dropped my bags off at the Karibuni Centre - an old Swedish mission station that would become my home for the next two nights - and went straight off with my new friends to one of their children's feeding programmes. It was being held at the Stable Pentecostal Church in Old Airport district, or Iyela. There, 107 four- to ten-year-olds had been waiting patiently for the arrival of their guest, and sang raucously to me when I arrived. Come to think of it now, their voices were so raucous that maybe they were shouting at me for being late.

One Pastor Maynard was orchestrating the event which, thankfully for the hungry children, didn't last long. After a simple greeting I was taken across the road to the Grassroots Centre where I was shown around and ate a tasty meal of rice, beans, spinach and banana – the same dish as the children were eating. We were joined by Dr Frank Anton, a young mental health and rehabilitation doctor who gives two days a week to the medical health care of the children. It was a little easier to talk with him, although the team were all still quite formal with me.

Eventually an older man, Pastor Yosiah, who is a trustee and original member of Stable Churches back in 1991, demonstrated that he could indeed speak good English. I wasn't feeling too good, with some heart fluttering and dizziness, but managed to draw them out a bit by asking about their families and their city.

I discovered that the local industry is (or was) the manufacture of iron sheets for roofs. Mbeya is big - home to almost 400,000 people - but appears to have no real centre as such. It's not as hilly (or as clean) as Kigali, but has a similar sort of feel, I thought to myself, or maybe a cross between Kigali and Ndola, with quite generous wide roads and a fairly laid-back feel to it.

After a little more time with the children, we set off again for another church, this time in a little building in Mabatini. We were warmly greeted by an excited Pastor Rose and their little choir, who were practising at the time, and sang us a couple of songs. I think they were settling in to sing us ten songs but, after two, Richard waved for them to stop. Tomorrow another one hundred children will be fed at this tiny little centre.

Back at the Karibuni Centre, I ate omelette and chips and drank black tea in the little restaurant run by the centre. More often than not, I eat alone in such places. But this evening, I shared the restaurant with a young couple who were staying here overnight, in transit from Malawi to Dar es Salaam.

"We are spending eight weeks in the region, travelling by bus", they told me in their English accents.

"Where are you from?" I asked.

"Oh, somewhere near Birmingham," they replied, as though I might have just about heard of England's second city. I pressed them further.

"I live in Stratford," said the girl. "And I am from Hereford," said the boy.

"Are you football fans?' I asked, and explained that I visit both those towns watching my team, Kettering Town, play.

"No. But I do know about Kettering Town though, from a comedian who sings a weird song about them as part of his act," she said with some enthusiasm.

I smiled. A somewhat distorted smile, exiting mouth left, and ending with a slight twitch. "We're talking about James Acaster, aren't we," I grimaced. "I used to babysit for him - or for his parents - when he was tiny. And by the way, Kettering fans don't actually sing the way he says they do. We tend to think he's a bit of an embarrassment."

I desperately wanted to redeem the image of Kettering Town by telling them that we were the first side in the UK to have sponsors on our shirt, and that we had scored more FA Cup goals than any other team in history, but my acute sense of discernment led me to detect that they weren't in the slightest bit interested. I finished my omelette in silence.

The following day I enjoyed the dedicated attention of Richard and his lovely young assistant, Happiness. As we drove to our first appointment, Richard told me about their work. We had begun to get the hang of each other's accents.

Grassroots feed 3,000 children every week, once a week, at fifteen of their 47 church centres. Although this is a significant programme, it is only one of a number of initiatives they have committed to in the area. About 2,000 children are sponsored throughout their schooling, and among their alumni was Happiness, who went on to university, where she studied law. They also do milk and egg distributions, improve the sanitation at schools, provide bore holes and water pumps in rural locations and were given a five-acre piece of land near the old airport to develop an agricultural training facility and housing for the homeless. Two smart little homes have recently been completed and are due to receive their first residents within a few weeks. They really have made a great difference in this community, and I became more and more impressed.

We made visits to feeding centres at the wonderfully named communities of Shewa, Nyibuko, Nsalaga, Masanga, Uyole Ya Kati and Swaya. Richard was convinced I would remember each village and location for years to come. "You surely won't need to write notes to remind yourself of where we've been. Each of these place name's role easily off the tongue, don't you find?" he asked with sincerity.

'Yes,' I thought to myself with equal conviction and pen still in hand. 'They role easily off the tongue and drop into the undergrowth, never to be recalled again.' I continued to write notes. To get to Swaya required quite a long drive, in time rather than in miles, purely because of the road conditions. But the large church centre was in a beautiful rural location in the hills, looking down into the valley then up to the old airport district of the town. There I met Pastor Patrick and about thirty children who had arrived ridiculously early for their anticipated lunchtime meal. At another location the local pastor had taught the children how to greet me. "Good afternoon, Mr White Man," they boldly chanted as one.

Returning to my accommodation, I was intrigued by the roar of a nearby crowd. Following the sound, I entered the grounds of Mzumbe University, where I discovered their football team playing in front of about 1,500 excited students on what was probably the world's most bobbly pitch.

That evening I spotted a notice pinned to the guest house wall. It worried me. 'Dear Guests,' it read. 'Please be aware that the dogs are out between 11pm and 5am'. I was due to leave for Zambia at 4.30 in the morning. And I'm not a dog lover. I'm grateful that dogs bring added protection to such places, but am not completely convinced that they can adequately discern between the unwanted arrival of thieves and the departure of paying guests. Maybe a receipt would have helped, but I hadn't received one. I roamed the site, looking for someone official with whom I could share my concerns and request a check out that didn't involve the loss of a couple of limbs to a rabid animal. But my search was in vain. The place had become deserted.

During the night, between fitful dreams of being torn to shreds by savage hounds, I woke to realise there was also a power cut and, to a backdrop of the barking and growling of the guard dogs, lay wondering how on earth I was going to gather all my belongings in the dark and to leave well before the sun had risen in Mumbai, yet alone in Mbeya. I felt like the proverbial agnostic dyslexic insomniac, who apparently lay awake all night wondering if there was a Dog.

I was up at 4.15, and gasped under a cold shower. The power had been restored and there was not a dog to be seen or heard. Why on earth do I worry so much? Someone had even kindly left me two boiled eggs, some bread and a flask of tea to send me on my way. I happily consumed them while waiting for the arrival of my new Tanzanian friends. Ahead of us was a long journey, 1,100km south-west, to Ndola, Zambia. It would take seventeen hours to complete.

Other books by Alan Cutting

Cutting Across the Borders (2018)

ISBN 978-1-7200-2050-9

My story leads you through my nervous but rescued childhood. It opens a door into the intensive community lifestyle that I lived in my twenties and thirties. And it tussles with the pain, betrayal and disasters that I encountered during my forties.

And the rest, as they *don't* tend to say, is geography.

I invite you to journey with me on the relentless, unusual and often extreme global adventures of my fifties and sixties. It's a story of people, of places and of relationships; a true and radical tale of love and passion, of disappointment, vulnerability and determination. And of rescue and grace, hope and faithfulness.

Raising Families: Envisioning the Church to Empower its Neighbourhood (2019)

ISBN 978-1-0914-1053-4

Alan Cutting heads up Raising Families, a 'Church and Community Mobilisation' process worked out in Africa and Central Asia. Through the 3,002 churches he has partnered with in the last six years, 59,681 families have seen significant, practical, quantifiable improvements to their lives - sickness averted, children in school, crops in the field and food on the table - and a total of 14,705 people have come through repentance and faith into a living relationship with God through Jesus Christ.

Writing with a UK Christian readership in mind, Alan anticipates that through this book, UK churches, small groups and individuals will learn much from these churches in other parts of the world, and will be stimulated in their own determination to engage in new, meaningful and Christ-like ways with their own communities and neighbourhoods in the UK.

Cutting Across the Generations (2020)

ISBN 979-8-6442-1124-1

This is the story of six generations of the Cutting family - farmers, doctors, clergymen and solicitors - all of whom lived in Suffolk and Norfolk between 1760 and 1985. What does this family have to do with Waterloo and the arrest of Napoleon, with three different Presidents of the USA, with leading abolitionists, with a highly decorated WW2 General in Nazi Germany, and with the career of England's World Cup winning football manager, Sir Alf Ramsey?

As we take a chronological walk through six generations of Cuttings, we will encounter all these notables and more, but will also have to face issues of smuggling, bankruptcy, gassing, sickness, and the tragic deaths of sons and daughters, through disease - and even in an avalanche.

Each character had their own unique circumstances to contend with, and passions to pursue. They all had their ups and downs, their strengths and weaknesses, their successes and failures, their idiosyncrasies and vulnerabilities. Collectively, their vocations, relationships, writings and travels help to build an intriguing picture of 200 years of East Anglian life, and of the conflicting stresses and strains of their times.

Printed in Great Britain
by Amazon